REVOR F KNIGHT

God's
Wonderful
Word

Introducing
each book
of the Bible

DayOne

© Day One Publications

First published by Day One Publications 2007

ISBN 978-1-84625-072-9

ISBN 978-1-84625-072-9

British Library Cataloguing in Publication Data available

Published by Day One Publications
Ryelands Road, Leominster, HR6 8NZ
☎ 01568 613 740 FAX 01568 611 473
email—sales@dayone.co.uk
web site—www.dayone.co.uk
North American—e-mail—sales@dayonebookstore.com
North American—web site—www.dayonebookstore.com

Printed by Gutenberg Press, Malta

Trevor Knight loves his Bible—and it shows! For any new Christian wanting to get an overall grasp of what Scripture says—and for other believers looking for a concise overview of the Bible as an incentive to further study—this book will be a heart-warming help.

Dr John Blanchard, internationally known Author, Evangelist, Conference Teacher and Apologist

Don't be deceived by the size of God's wonderful Word. In it are gems that have been presented to us on a plate. This is a treasure-trove of biblical insight and instruction which will be repeatedly read and referred to. I am delighted that this is being republished.

Roger Carswell, Evangelist and Author

I am delighted that a high quality publisher like Day One is taking over the excellent little book, God's wonderful Word, *for a brilliant communicator like Trevor Knight. That is a winning combination! When I recommended this book as one of only six in* The Bible Panorama, *my only regret was that it would have limited circulation. Now this 'encouraging, quickly readable, concise, clear and simple introductory guide', through Day One, will be able to benefit all Christians—especially those new to serious Bible reading—throughout the English-speaking world.*

Gerard Chrispin, Director, Daylight Christian Ministries

This is no ordinary book. Each book of the Bible is summarized into two pages. No effort has been spared to ensure that each summary is crystal clear. It is a precious book from the pen of one who writes with the passion of a preacher, the precision of a mathematician and the helpfulness of a great teacher.

Dr David Norbury, General Secretary of the Evangelical Movement of Wales

Trevor has always had the remarkable gift of making the Bible come alive through his unique ability to portray the characters and main thrust of the themes in the Bible. A noted Bible Teacher who has seen many turn to Christ under his ministry over more than

Commendations

a generation, I heartily recommend Trevor's ministry through these pages to many more who want to have a thorough introduction to the wonder of Scripture.

Professor Andy McIntosh DSc, FIMA, C.Math, FEI, C.Eng, FInstP, MIGEM, FRAeS, University of Leeds, Creation speaker, author and apologist

The widespread disappearance of the 'Quiet Time' amongst younger evangelicals is beginning to impoverish the church. We desperately need to get the next generation of Christians into the Bible and the Bible into them. Trevor Knight's excellent book is a heart-warming, practical and realistic response to this need. It is ideal for students and I warmly and unhesitatingly recommend its widest use

Richard Cunningham Director of UCCF (The Christian Unions), UK

Contents

Have you ever wondered what a gold mine looks like? It is probably very ordinary, and possibly even uninviting.

The Bible is God's gold mine. Outwardly, it may look a very ordinary book. To some, it may even look uninviting. But the treasures to be found inside are really thrilling. Time spent in 'prospecting' its pages is always amply rewarded. To help you glimpse some of God's 'gold' to be found there is the purpose of this book.

And have you ever looked at the sky on a clear night and tried to count the stars? We know that there are so many that it is impossible to count them all, but it is also true that the longer we look, the more stars we seem to see.

The Bible is like that. The truths and treasures it contains cannot really be numbered, yet those who read it regularly will tell you that the more they do so, the more they see. The following pages have been written to help you spot some of God's 'shining blessings' to be discovered there.

I wonder whether you have heard the following story?

A girl was once given a book as a present. She found it rather boring, and put it to one side before she had finished reading it. Years later, a young man fell in love with her. She was surprised to learn that he was the author of the long-neglected book. She went home to read it with renewed interest. This time, it seemed so wonderful. Knowing the author made all the difference.

And so it is with the Bible.

Many neglect it. Some make the mistake of thinking it is boring. Too often the trouble is that such people do not 'know the Author'. It is God's book. It is about God's Son, and how he 'came into the world to save sinners' (1 Timothy 1:15).

We need to know Christ as a personal Saviour if we really want to discover what the Bible is all about. If you are not a converted Christian yet, before studying the Bible or reading this book any further, turn to Christ in prayer. Ask him to do the miracle in your heart that he has done for so many others. The following words may help you:

Dear Lord, I realize that the Bible has so much to teach me about you. And yet, without you and your help, I will never properly understand what it is all about. I know it tells of your love for me, and of your death for my sins. Help me, right now, to turn from my sins, and to receive you as my Saviour.

And then teach me about yourself Lord, and how I should follow you day by day, as I regularly read your holy Word. Amen.

And so ...

with Christ in your heart
and the Bible in your hand
(and this book by your side for reference!) ...
may you know the thrill of discovering God's 'gold' in
'God's wonderful Word!'

T.F.K.

Many people who read the Bible daily find it helpful to have a notebook or diary in which to write a thought for the day.

The first Bible I bought after becoming a Christian rapidly became full of daily thoughts recorded in different coloured ballpoint pens. Alas! I soon discovered that the ink from these pens discoloured the pages! Soon afterwards, my fiancée bought me a wide-margined Bible for Christmas. How wonderful to have extra space to write in daily thoughts—this time making sure I used pencil or different ink! Years of use meant it eventually had to be replaced. Various Bibles and loose-leaf notebooks have been used since then. I still prefer to jot down thoughts in my Bible in pencil each morning, but later I transfer them to my laptop 'Bible online' for a more permanent record.

It is good to aim to read the whole Bible through in a year—if you are daunted by this prospect, try reading the whole of the New Testament in your first year, and the Old Testament in a second year. In this way, you will succeed in reading the whole of God's Word in two years.

One person who gained increasing delight from reading his Bible was George Müller, famous for founding the Ashley Down orphanages near Bristol. He said:

The first three years after conversion I neglected the Word of God. Since I began to search it diligently the blessing has been wonderful.

I have read the Bible through one hundred times and always with increasing delight. Each time it seems like a new book to me.

Great has been the blessing from consecutive, diligent, daily study. I look upon it as a lost day when I have not had a good time over the Word of God.

The 'Quiet Time' is a name given to the Christian's daily devotional time with God. Many will testify to it being the greatest source of blessing in their Christian lives. There is no substitute for it. It is the key to spiritual health and growth.

As the name suggests, the first things to sort out are a quiet 'time' and 'place' where you can be undisturbed with the Saviour. Jesus taught about going into your room privately and shutting the door, in order to have a prayer time (Matthew 6:6).

For the average Christian, home is usually quiet in the early morning, before the rest of the family get up. If you have your own room, all well and good; otherwise, choose a place where you think you will be undisturbed.

There is a lot to be said for washing, dressing and even having a cup of tea or coffee before you begin. Such practices shake off drowsiness, clear the mind and prepare you for a time of thoughtful devotion.

Be sensible about distractions: avoid uncomfortable chairs and Bibles in which the small print is a strain on the eyes, and never, ever yield to the temptation to look at the morning's post or paper first—it can prove disastrous! Time can speed by on these things and squeeze out the vital time with God.

Make sure that you have Bible, pen or pencil, any notebook for daily thoughts and your prayer list within easy reach. You will not want to be disturbed by having to leave the room to get them.

Start with a brief prayer asking God's blessing on your time. Next, read the Bible passage you have decided on. Choose a scheme of reading, and stick to it. Do not wander at random from one Bible passage to another.

Before starting to read any book in the Bible, it will be helpful to have a bird's-eye-view gained from the 'Know the book' section for it (see, for example, pages 16–17). It will also help to read 'Mark these words' in case you want to underline various words as you come across them in your Bible reading. Although the questions are based on the New King James version, they can be easily adapted to suit other Bible versions. Although it is not essential, you may find it worthwhile investing in a wide-margined Bible for working through these questions.

Make as many notes as you wish in your notebook or margin of your Bible, but aim at getting at least one thought for the day to be remembered and shared with others.

Next, pray about what you have read, and how it relates to both yourself and others.

When you have finished this time of private prayer and praise, turn to your prayer diary and have a time of specific intercession for others. Some may have special needs over which you can linger. On other occasions you may adopt Paul's encouraging words, 'making mention of you', and commit these people in brief prayer to the Lord for his blessing.

To summarize what has been said:

(a) Make sure you go to a private place, on time, with all that you need.

(b) Pray briefly for God's guidance and blessing.

(c) Read your Bible passage for that day.

(d) Decide on and write down your thought for the day.

(e) Pray about matters arising from your Bible reading.

(f) Turn to your prayer list, and pray for others.

William Booth, who founded the Salvation Army, once wrote in his diary:

I do promise God that I will rise early every morning to have minutes—no less than five—in private prayer. I will endeavour to conduct myself as a humble, meek, and zealous follower of Jesus, and by serious witness and warning, I will try to lead others to think of the needs of their immortal souls. I hereby vow to read no less than four chapters in God's Word each day. I will cultivate a spirit of self-denial and will yield myself a prisoner of love to the Redeemer of the world.

Somebody once wittily listed the following guidelines, indicating how the Quiet Time should NOT be conducted!

Ten rules for effortless Bible reading

1. Always read at night when you are tired.

2. Open at random: your chances of striking a genealogy are pretty good.

3. Never read more than five verses at a time: you might get the idea of the story.

4. Tackle the most difficult passages first: they will encourage you to give up more quickly.
5. Don't have a system: you might know where to start.
6. Fill your bookshelves with translations: they prove it's too hard to understand.
7. Never make notes: you might remember something.
8. Never share what you have read with others: speech often brings thoughts into focus.
9. Never attempt a group Bible study: confusion might disappear.
10. Whatever you do, never, ever become a regular daily reader: it might affect the way you live.

Summaries of each Bible book, together with related exercises, occur in the following pages. The order is the same as that in which the books occur in the Old and New Testament.

I believe the Bible is the best gift God has ever given to man. All the good from the Saviour of the world is communicated to us through this book.

Abraham Lincoln.

Reading the Bible through in a year

I supposed I knew my Bible,
     Reading piecemeal, hit or miss,
Now a bit of John or Matthew,
     Now a snatch of Genesis,
Certain chapters of Isaiah,
     Certain Psalms (the twenty-third),
Twelfth of Romans, first of Proverbs
     Yes, I thought I knew the Word!
But I found that thorough reading
     Was a different thing to do,
And the way was unfamiliar
     When I read the Bible through.

You who like to play at Bible,
     Dip and dabble here and there,
Just before you kneel, aweary,
     And yawn through a hurried prayer,
You who treat the crown of writings
     As you treat no other book—
Just a paragraph disjointed,
     Just a crude, impatient look—
Try a worthier procedure,
     Try a broad and steady view;
You will kneel in very rapture,
     When you read the Bible through!

Anonymous

Part 1: The Old Testament

At the coronation of each new British monarch, the Archbishop of Canterbury makes a presentation of a copy of the Holy Bible, saying:

We present you with this Book, the most valuable thing that this world affords. Here is wisdom; this is the Royal Law; these are the lively oracles of God.

Someone else has said,

The Bible is the divinely inspired volume in which God has revealed to mankind the truths which make for their highest well-being, here and hereafter, which he has not revealed to them otherwise, and which they could not have discovered by their own reason and research.

God's *authority* is stamped on every page, with 'thus says the LORD' occurring over 2,000 times.

God's *autograph* can be detected in prophecy—for only he has the ability to record history in advance.

God's *answer* to the human problem of sin is to be found in his redeeming Son. The Bible is primarily his story. The Old Testament anticipates his coming, but the unanswered question throughout its pages is 'Where is the Lamb?' (Genesis 22:7).

That question is answered in the New Testament, when the last prophet of the old covenant pointed to Christ and said, 'Behold! The Lamb of God' (John 1:29).

This is the Book that can introduce you to the Saviour, and gain you an entrance to heaven. Do not neglect it.

Reuben Torrey said,

Many a life that has been barren and unsatisfied has become rich and useful through the introduction into it of regular, persevering, daily study of the Bible. This study may not be very interesting at first; the results may not be very encouraging, but if one will keep pegging away, it will soon begin to count as nothing else has ever counted in the development of character, and in the enrichment of the whole life. Nothing short of absolute physical inability should be allowed to interfere with this daily study.

Genesis

Know the book

Genesis is a book of *revelation*. Just as God revealed to John how everything will eventually end, recorded for us in the last book of the Bible, so God revealed to Moses how everything began, recorded for us in this first book of the Bible.

Genesis is a book of *prose*. It is not poetry. It is a book of facts—not myths.

Genesis is a book of *introduction*. All the facts, truths and revelations of the Bible are here in embryo. It is the seedbed of the entire Word of God, and essential to the true understanding of its every part.

Genesis is a book of *beginnings*. It tells us about the beginnings of the universe, life, man, marriage, sin, death, redemption, cities, nations, languages, music, literature, art, agriculture, etc. In fact it tells us about the beginning of almost everything—except God. It is a book that begins with God already there at the beginning. For the person who wants to begin with God, it is an excellent book to start with.

Genesis is a book of *truth*. Its early verses quickly point out the falsehoods of atheism, polytheism, pantheism, the eternal existence of matter, and evolution. Its early chapters soon tell of man falling, although placed in a perfect environment (so much for the teaching of humanism!). The first man who was born became a murderer—highlighting the nature of fallen man—while the first man who died went to heaven—highlighting the mercy of a gracious God (see the story of Cain and Abel in ch. 4).

The first section shows the spread of sin and corruption from the individual life (ch. 3) to the family (ch. 4-5), then to society (ch. 6–10) and to all nations (ch. 11). The second section then shows how God steps in to remedy the situation, dealing first with an individual (Abraham) and then with his family, until all nations are offered the 'salvation' provided at the time of Joseph.

The patriarchs (or 'fathers') of the Hebrew race were Abraham, Isaac and Jacob.

Abraham was tested regarding obedience (ch. 12), values (ch. 13), love and loyalty (ch. 14), and faith (ch. 15–21); he was given the severest test of all (ch. 22), and was even tested in his final years (ch. 22–25). He triumphed gloriously and was honoured in being called 'the friend of God' (James 2:23).

Isaac is a wonderful parallel or picture of the Lord Jesus Christ:

(a) The miraculous birth of the promised son (ch. 21).

(b) The sacrificial offering of the beloved son (ch. 22).

(c) The father seeking a bride for the exalted son (ch. 24).

Joseph is another picture of Christ. When you read Genesis, note the chapters showing him as (a) the favourite son, (b) the suffering servant, (c) the exalted saviour.

MARK THESE WORDS

1. In chapter 1 underline each 'then God said', and connect it with the following 'and it was so'. Notice the power of God's word, and see how Psalm 33:9 is an apt summary for this chapter.

2. Ten 'family histories' are given in Genesis, marked by the words, 'this is the history of' or 'this is the genealogy of'. Find them, and mark them in chapters 2, 5, 6, 10, 11 (twice), 25 (twice), 36 and 37.

3. The Christian at death is not taken from family and friends so much as 'gathered to his people'. This phrase occurs 4 times in Genesis. Whose deaths are described in this way? Find and underline the words in chapters 25 (twice), 35 and 49.

4. It is interesting to note the first time certain words occur in the Bible. Underline the following 'firsts': 'come' (ch. 7), 'drunk' (ch. 9), 'war' (ch. 14), and 'believed' (ch. 15).

Exodus

Know the book

Exodus opens with the birth of Moses, where Genesis closes with the death of Joseph. About two hundred years separate these events. The twelve tribes of Israel have expanded numerically, but have been forced into the role of immigrant slave labour.

In Genesis, God created a world for himself. In Exodus, he now redeems a people for himself. The book starts with a groan (2:24) and ends with glory (40:34). In between, God in his goodness and grace (see 34:6) first leads the people into liberty, and then into spirituality.

'Exodus' means 'way out'. It is an apt title for the book. It has been called the *Pilgrim's Progress* of the Old Testament. Every person who trusts Christ for salvation finds many of the lessons in Exodus repeated in his or her own experience.

Exodus contains three outstanding events: the exodus from Egypt, the receiving of the law, and the building of the tabernacle.

CH. 1–18 THE WAY TO LIBERTY

CH. 19–24 THE WAY TO BEHAVE

CH. 25–40 THE WAY TO WORSHIP

God's method of saving the people is through a man. Moses is first saved himself, then schooled (ch. 2). Later, he excuses himself when confronted with God's call by pleading that he has no ability (3:11), no message (3:13), no authority (4:1), no eloquence (4:10) and no inclination (4:13). D. L. Moody said that Moses spent forty years in the palace learning to be somebody, forty years in the desert learning to be nobody, and then forty years learning what God can do with a nobody. What an encouragement to us today!

The plagues were miraculous, as shown by their unusual season, unusual degree, and immediate response to Moses' commands.

At Passover (ch. 12) the firstborn were saved on the basis of faith in the blood of a lamb. In Genesis, Abel had offered the blood of a lamb (Genesis

4) and Abraham had been accepted on the basis of faith (Genesis 15). It is becoming increasingly clear that salvation is on the faith–blood basis. The law is given to inform of sin, and restrict sin, but not to provide another way of salvation from sin. The moral commands should still govern our behaviour, whereas the ceremonial aspects were prophetic types of Christ, and have been superseded by his coming and death.

The third section of Exodus is full of earthly things with heavenly meanings. The high priest's clothes and their colours have much to teach of Christ. The tabernacle furniture, in order from the entrance, deals with blood atonement, washing, entrance, fellowship, illumination, intercession, and the ark and mercy seat beyond the veil. Think it over. That order is still the way to worship today.

MARK THESE WORDS

1. Underline 'the Lord said' in chapters 3–12 (near the beginning of each chapter). Other chapters have it too.
2. Note the 7 'I will's in 6:6–8.
3. Find the 7 occasions God says 'Let my people go' (ch. 5–10).
4. Ring 'a', 'the' and 'your' before the word 'lamb' in 12:3–5.
5. The Ten Commandments are meant to be obeyed personally. Underline each 'you' and 'your' in them (20:3–17).
6. Moses obeyed the Lord in the small detail. Ring the word 'all' in 40:16, and then underline the 7 occasions in the rest of the chapter where it says, 'as the Lord commanded Moses'.
7. Draw a plan of the tabernacle and its furniture, with the ark in the Most Holy Place, 3 items in the Holy Place, 2 items in the compound, and the entrances on the east. Label all the items in your diagram.

Leviticus

Know the book
The first five books of the Bible were written by Moses and are referred to as the Pentateuch. Leviticus is the central book of these five, and its contents form the very heart of their message. Leviticus 19:2 is an apt summary: 'You shall be holy for I the LORD your God am holy.'

In Genesis, we read of man ruined; in Exodus, we read of him redeemed; in Leviticus, we find him worshipping.

In Exodus, God had prepared a *place* for worship (the tabernacle). In Leviticus, God reveals the *pattern* for worship. No longer are the people viewed as sinners in need of union—they are viewed as saints in need of communion.

CH. 1–16 THE WAY TO GOD (SACRIFICE)

CH. 17–23 THE WALK WITH GOD (SANCTIFICATION)

For the Christian the way of getting clean, and keeping clean, is summarized in 1 John 1:7: 'If we walk in the light as he is in the light, we have fellowship with one another, and the blood of Jesus Christ his Son cleanses us from all sin.'

Leviticus often uses the word 'atonement', meaning 'cover'. The blood shed on the altar in Leviticus could only 'cover' sin, until Christ shed his blood on the cross, paying the real price that God demanded for sin's cleansing.

Not all the blood of beasts	But Christ, the heavenly Lamb,
On Jewish altars slain,	Takes all our sins away;
Could give the guilty conscience peace	A sacrifice of nobler name,
Or wash away the stain.	And richer blood than they.

Isaac Watts

The book of Hebrews in the New Testament is an explanatory commentary on the book of Leviticus. Writing after Christ's death on the cross, John refers to the feasts in Leviticus not as 'the feasts of the LORD' but as the feasts 'of the Jews' (John 2:13; 5:1; 7:2; etc.).

The first seven chapters deal with the five offerings: Burnt, Grain, Peace, Sin and Trespass (the first letters help memorization as they are in alphabetical order). The first two emphasize complete consecration, the central one is of cloudless communion, and the last two emphasize continued cleansing. These are experiences the Christian should still maintain today.

'Cleanliness is part of godliness'—for this book confronts us with the need for clean foods (ch. 11), bodies (ch. 12), clothes (ch. 13), houses (ch. 14) and contacts (ch. 15), as well as clean leaders (ch. 8–10), and a clean nation (ch. 16). The two largest chapters in the centre of the book deal with leprosy and its cleansing. Defilement from this disease can be in flesh, head, clothes or home (ch. 13–14).

The emphasis of the offerings is 'Get right with God'. The feasts are a reminder to 'Keep right with God'. There are seven feasts (ch. 23) but only three that all the people gathered to celebrate: Passover (typifying the death of Christ), the feast fifty days afterwards at the beginning of harvest, later known as Pentecost (the coming of the Holy Spirit), and Tabernacles (the final harvest at the end of the world).

Leviticus starts by stressing complete dedication; it finishes in chapter 40 by dealing with the tithe (the tenth part that belongs to God).

MARK THESE WORDS
1. Choose one or more of the following words, and ring them each time they appear in the book: 'blood' (80+), 'holiness/holy' (80+), 'atonement' (40+).
2. Underline 'the LORD spoke'—words which start 20 chapters, and occur in over 30 other places. Count how many you find.
3. Ring 'it shall be forgiven' in chapters 4–6 (9 times).
4. Ring each 'if' and 'I will' in chapter 26, noticing carefully which 'if' governs which 'I will'.
5. Underline the last 11 words of 17:11 and memorize them. Compare with the last 8 words of Hebrews 9:22.

Numbers

Know the book

Numbers resumes the story of the Israelites' journey where Exodus left off.

Numbers is a book of service. It correctly follows Exodus and Leviticus, because only the saved and worshipping soul is qualified for service. In the early part of the book every Israelite is allocated his position and job. 1 Corinthians 12 indicates that every Christian has a position and job within the people of God. When God calls to a task, he also equips. Notice that the carts were not shared out equally among the Levites, but they were shared out fairly, because some had more difficult tasks than others (see Numbers 7:1–9).

Numbers is also a book of failure. God's purpose in bringing the people out of Egypt was that he might bring them into the Promised Land. Failure was tragic, and it is an apt warning to Christians to make sure they maintain wholehearted following. We are also confronted with individual failures by Miriam and Aaron (ch. 12), the ten spies (ch. 13), Korah, Dathan and Abiram (ch. 16–17), as well as Moses (ch. 20). Read Hebrews 4:1 to see the relevance for today.

Numbers is also a book of murmurings. This is the prominent sin of the central chapters. Grumbling is not a little sin. Those who murmur without cause will soon have cause to murmur.

Numbers is also a book of wanderings. The people numbered in the first census (ch. 1) spent almost forty years in the wilderness dying off at well over 100 a day. They went round in circles getting nowhere. Their lives were wasted. To avoid a similar mistake, Christians should make their life's motto: 'The will of God, nothing more, nothing less, nothing else, always, everywhere and whatever the cost.'

After getting organized (ch. 1–14) and getting sidetracked for thirty-eight years (ch. 15–20), they eventually get on target again (ch. 21–36). This requires a second census for the new generation involved (ch. 26).

The Saviour said, 'Moses … wrote about me' (John 5:46). This fourth book of Moses contains further types or pictures of Christ: note the rock which had to be 'smitten' to bring lifesaving blessing to people (20:7–11), the bronze serpent lifted up on a pole, so that whoever wanted to might 'look and live' (21:4–9), and the cities of refuge providing sanctuary for the guilty from the avenger hot on his heels (ch. 35).

Extensive space is devoted to Balaam (ch. 22–25), who could be called 'The mercenary prophet'. Even an ass could see what he couldn't! Although he could not get God to be unfaithful to his people, he suggested a method of getting the people to be unfaithful to their God (31:16). Those who are trying to make a 'profit' out of religion are often blind, compromising, and a strange mixture of truth and untrustworthiness.

MARK THESE WORDS

1. Notice the continuing authority of God's Word. Underline as many examples of 'the LORD spoke to Moses' as you can find (over 40).
2. In chapter 3 the Levites become the 'blood-bought' tribe instead of the firstborn. Ring each 'instead of' (4 times).
3. Chapters 11–21 contain eight complainings about the way, the food, the leaders, the giants, the land, the priesthood, the thirst and the provision. Put a star by each one, when found.
4. Ring each 'besides' and 'regular burnt offering' in chapter 28.
5. Ring each 'murderer' and 'manslayer' in 35:15–34. What careful distinction does the Bible make in using these terms?

Deuteronomy

Know the book

Deuteronomy is the last of the five books of Moses. For that reason the Jews called it the 'five fifths of the law'.

'Deuteronomy' is derived from two Hebrew words meaning 'second law'. Moses does not give new laws in this book, he merely restates the old laws for the benefit of a new generation. The forty years' wilderness wandering had seen the death of one generation, and the rising of another. The new people are faced now with a new situation: they are about to enter a new land and a new era, but they must keep to the old standards. 'Take heed to yourselves, lest you forget ...' (4:23).

Deuteronomy was written by Moses when he had less than one month to live. What a legacy he left! It kindled revival in the time of Josiah (2 Kings 23) and Ezra (Nehemiah 8), and was quoted by Christ in conquering temptation (Matthew 4). At the end of his life the apostle Paul also turned to writing to bless people (Philippians 3:1). It is never too late to be a blessing.

Deuteronomy emphasizes one aspect of God that crowns all that has been revealed so far in the Bible. Genesis indicated his sovereignty, Exodus his power in redemption, Leviticus his holiness, and Numbers his righteousness—now we are told his actions were motivated 'because he loved' (Deuteronomy 4:37).

Deuteronomy consists mainly of four speeches by Moses. The first reminds the people of how good God has been in past history (ch. 1–4); the second is a reminder of the laws already given, which they should observe (ch. 5–26); the third summarizes what will happen depending on their response (ch. 27–28); and the last contains a new covenant and an exhortation to make sure they choose wisely (ch. 29–30). How apt are such reminders and warnings for us as well.

The concluding chapters deal with four final charges by Moses (ch. 31); a song of Moses (ch. 32); the final blessing of Moses (ch. 33); and the epitaph of Moses (ch. 34), probably written by Joshua, his successor.

CH. 1–4 Looking back

CH. 5–26 Looking on

CH. 27–34 Looking out!

The grand chapters in this book teach both the vital and the incidental. Rumours can be squashed, according to Dr Maclean of Bath, by asking six questions based on Deuteronomy 13:14: Have you 'enquired'? Have you 'searched out'? Have you 'asked diligently'? Is it true? Is it certain? Is it something which has happened?

Deuteronomy 18 contains the prophecy of the great prophet (Christ). Deuteronomy 28 contains an astounding detailed prophecy of the Jews and their history—fulfilled when the warning here went unheeded.

Deuteronomy has eight references to 'signs and wonders'. This is the most found in any Old Testament book and equals the number of times they are mentioned in Acts; together they provide the Bible student with a very balanced view of what God has done at outstanding times in history. Sadly, the tragic history of the Jews was to be another 'sign and wonder' (28:46).

MARK THESE WORDS

1. Ring each 'love' you find. Draw an arrow in the margin to show if it is from God (downwards), for God (upwards), or for other people (horizontal).
2. Ring each 'with all your heart', and note what should be done this way: 4:29; 10:12; 13:3; 30:2 and 30:10.
3. Choose one of the following words, ring them each time they occur, and count how many you find: 'hear' (30); 'keep' (39); 'do' (about 100).
4. Note what the 3 'therefore's in chapter 11 are 'there for'.
5. Note that John Newton placed 15:15 over his mantelpiece.

Joshua

Know the book

Joshua was the man chosen to succeed Moses. He was born in Egypt, trained under Moses, was spiritual (see Exodus 33:11), an active helper (Exodus 17:10), and one of the two faithful spies (Numbers 14:6).

Joshua was originally called 'Oshea' (Numbers 13:8). The meaning of his name reminds us that we have to be 'saved' before we can be a 'saviour'.

Joshua led the Israelites into the Promised Land. In this, as well as in his name, he is a picture or type of Christ. Moses, Aaron and Miriam all died before entering the Promised Land. They represent law, priesthood and prophets, which may do much for us but cannot do what the 'Saviour' alone can do.

In the books of Moses, the Israelites were introduced to a redeemed position; in Joshua, they enter a redeemed experience. The last book of Moses is one of anticipation; Joshua is one of realization. In the former we see a vision of faith; in the latter we see a venture of faith. The early chapters of Joshua deal with their getting fully into the land; the central chapters with their getting on top of their enemies; and the final chapters with them sorting out their shared responsibilities.

CH. 1–5 ENTERING THE LAND

CH. 6–12 CONQUERING THE LAND

CH. 13–24 DIVIDING THE LAND

Songs we call 'Negro spirituals' often refer to the 'Promised Land' as meaning heaven, and our journey through life as our pilgrimage there. Such thoughts may have been consoling in the days of tragic slavery, but in the Bible Canaan is not a type of heaven, but rather of the victorious life every Christian should experience while on earth.

The promise to the Israelites was of all material blessings on earth in Abraham; the promise to Christians is of all 'spiritual blessings in the heavenly places in Christ' (Ephesians 1:3).

Joshua was told that he must daily study the part of 'the Bible' he had. Obedience would lead to blessing (Joshua 1:8).

Rahab was saved by faith (Hebrews 11:31) and a scarlet thread (Joshua 2:18). The scarlet theme of blood runs through the whole Bible.

The Red Sea experience had got the Israelites 'out' of Egypt; the Jordan crossing got them 'in' to where they should be; there followed a day of updating neglected duties (5:7). Such times are still vital.

Success started with the miracle of Jericho; Joshua used strategy to conquer thereafter—miracles and methods are complementary.

There are a few failures in this book: the covetousness of Achan (ch. 7); prayerlessness over the Gibeonites (ch. 9); and compromise with those they should have conquered (16:10).

Moses used his last days to write a book; Joshua used his to have a leaders' conference (ch. 24).

MARK THESE WORDS

1. Ring 'be strong and of good courage' (4 times in ch. 1).
2. Note what Joshua had to do each day (1:8) and how he conquered in the mornings: 3:1; 6:12; 7:16 and 8:10. Determine to follow his example.
3. Underline Rahab's prayer that her family be saved (ch. 2). Are you praying regularly for your family and friends?
4. Ring 'I saw … coveted … took … hid' in 7:21.
5. Who 'wholly followed the LORD'? Ring the words in chapter 14 (3 times).
6. Chapter 10 teaches thoroughness. Ring each 'utterly destroyed' and count them.

Judges

Know the book

Judges is the Old Testament book of the 'Dark Ages'. After forty years in the wilderness, Joshua had introduced the people to early years of victory in Canaan. After his death, there was a rapid decline. Victory gave place to defeat, freedom to bondage, progress to declension, faith to unbelief, and unity to anarchy. It was a period of mixed fortunes with widespread failure that lasted for approximately 400 years.

Judges starts with compromise, and ends in corruption and calamity. At the beginning the people of God are fighting the foes, but by the end they are fighting one another. Initially they are under the rule of God (theocracy); by the end they are under the rule of nobody (anarchy—see 17:6). This situation leads later to them desiring to be under the rule of a king (monarchy).

Judges is the name given to the occasional leaders God raised up to rule during these times. Their influence was local rather than national. Their tasks were to fight the foes without, and settle the quarrels within. They illustrate Paul's words in 1 Corinthians 1:26: 'Not many wise according to the flesh, not many mighty, not many noble, are called.' All had weaknesses:

Othniel was young in years; Ehud was left-handed; Shamgar fought with an ox goad; Deborah was a woman; Gideon was from an obscure family; Jephthah was scorned for illegitimate birth; and Samson who was so strong was yet the weakest of them all when it came to morals.

Judges contains the recorded history of six apostasies. Each forms a cycle of experiences: sin leads to slavery, slavery to sorrow, sorrow to supplication (prayer), and supplication to salvation. Even in the 'Dark Ages' God was still ready to respond to prayer and deliver his people. The book therefore teaches that we should not presume, but neither should we despair. Sadly, the final depths are reached in the book not by external defeat, but by internal degradation. Wesley wisely said: 'But worst of all my foes I fear the enemy within.' So should we.

Each judge has lessons for us. Samson was the most promising individually. He was dedicated as a Nazirite, but toyed with his separation. He was the only one forsaken by the Lord. His only recorded prayer was that he might die with others. 'The grey-haired saint may fail at last.' We need to learn from his mistake.

Infidelity is the keynote of chapters 17 and 18. They contain a corrupt man, a corrupt mother, and corrupt money, ministry and might.

Immorality is the keynote of chapters 19, 20 and 21. They contain a corrupt maiden, corrupt men and corrupt morals. Wrong beliefs always precede wrong behaviour.

CH. 1–2 COMPROMISE

CH. 3–16 CONQUERED

CH. 17–21 CORRUPTION

MARK THESE WORDS

1. The first chapter contains 8 incomplete conquests. Ring the words 'did not' and 'nor did'.
2. Note the groaning in 2:18. That was much like the situation before they were redeemed (Exodus 2:24).
3. God can use weak points to prove us. Ring 'test' 3 times between 2:22 and 3:4.
4. 'Not by might, nor by power, but by my Spirit …' (Zechariah 4:6). Which 4 judges are we told God's Spirit came on?
5. For each of the 6 apostasies, look for a verse that shows each of the different experiences of 'sin', 'slavery', 'sorrow and supplication', and 'salvation'.

Ruth

Know the book

Ruth follows Judges in the Bible, but its story takes place during the tragic times under those leaders. It is like an oasis of purity in a desert of corruption. Here we read of peace instead of war, kindness instead of cruelty, and high ideals amid prevalent low morals. The word 'love' never occurs in it, yet love and devotion mark every chapter.

Ruth is one of only two books in the Bible which have as their titles the names of women. The other is Esther. Ruth was a Gentile who married a Hebrew husband; Esther was a Jewess who married a Gentile husband. Christians need not necessarily marry within their own race, but the Bible makes clear that for them it should be 'only in the Lord'—1 Corinthians 7:39.

Ruth contains the story of a prodigal family. Naomi went out of the land 'full', but came 'home again empty' (1:21). Her widowed daughter-in-law accompanies her 'empty', but is rewarded with a 'full measure' of blessing.

CH. 1 LOVE'S CHOICE

CH. 2 LOVE'S WORK

CH. 3 LOVE'S VENTURE

CH. 4 LOVE'S REWARD

Ruth contains an analogy of Christ in Boaz, the kinsman-redeemer who redeems to himself a Gentile bride. The early books of the Bible have already portrayed Christ in people (such as Joshua), events (like the bronze serpent), institutions (the Passover), offices (the prophet—like Moses) and actions (the striking of the rock to obtain what was needed to save lives)—now, we can see many aspects of the coming Christ, as kinsman-redeemer.

Every time that the book of Ruth uses the word 'kinsman', it is the Hebrew word 'goel'—meaning to free or to redeem. The kinsman-redeemer had to be (a) a blood relative, with (b) the power to redeem, (c) the willingness to pay, and (d) the willingness to accept the bride-to-be. Christ fulfilled every condition to be our Redeemer.

Ruth is a book which introduces us to the family tree of David and thereby 'David's greater Son' (Christ). These four chapters were read each year at early harvest (Pentecost). They were most appropriate, as Pentecost in Acts 2 commenced the all-inclusive offer of the gospel to both Jews and Gentiles.

For further meditation, Naomi can be considered as a picture of a saint backsliding; Orpah as a sinner rejecting; and Ruth as a sinner believing and blessed. Ruth also has many lessons for single womanhood regarding where to live, whom to live with, what to do, and how to behave.

MARK THESE WORDS

1. Ring 'kinsman' each time it occurs (13 times).
2. Ruth chose the same road, residence, relations, religion and resting place as Naomi. Underline 1:16–17, which tells us this.
3. Ring each 'redeem' in chapter 4.
4. Ruth is a book which starts with a sob, and ends with a song. Can you recall another book, already dealt with, that follows this same pattern?
5. Ruth is the *book* of the virtuous woman; Proverbs 31 is the *chapter* of the virtuous woman. Read Proverbs 31:10-31 and see how many 'points' that are mentioned there Ruth scores.
6. Read Matthew 1, and ring the names of 4 women in the family tree of Christ. Were the others as virtuous as Ruth?

1 Samuel

Know the book

1 Samuel deals with the last of the judges—Samuel—and introduces the first of the kings—Saul.

1 Samuel is the first book of three pairs of books which together deal with the whole history of the monarchy—a period of about 500 years. The monarchy is divided into three periods:

(a) A united kingdom for 120 years.

(b) A divided kingdom, resulting from civil war. The kingdom of Israel was in the north, and the kingdom of Judah was in the south. They had intermittent war and peace for 250 years, until Israel was conquered and taken into captivity by Assyria.

(c) A single kingdom of Judah which continued for over another century before being conquered and taken into captivity by Babylon.

After years in captivity, some Jews returned to their land, but a further 500 years passed before the birth of the Saviour—the heavenly King of kings, whose reign will never come to an end.

> CH. 1–8 ELI AND SAMUEL
>
> CH. 9–15 SAMUEL AND SAUL
>
> CH. 16–31 SAUL AND DAVID

The previous book, Ruth, dealt with a godly single woman. 1 Samuel starts with Hannah, a godly childless wife. In answer to her prayers a baby boy is born. She names him Samuel, meaning 'asked of God'. Samuel is dedicated to God, and grows to be one of the two people God marks out specially as men of prayer (see Jeremiah 15:1). It is his task to anoint Saul as the first king.

Saul was a man of muscle, but also a man of moods. He was a king who played the fool. 1 Samuel records his rise, reign and ruin.

Saul was humble to begin with (15:17) but gave way to presumption (ch. 13), rashness (ch. 14), disobedience (ch. 15), and even infidelity (ch. 28), because when heaven was silent, he turned to the forbidden provinces of mediums and the occult for help.

By contrast, his New Testament namesake—Saul of Tarsus, who became the apostle Paul—was wrong in the beginning and right at the end.

The second half of 1 Samuel deals with David. Chosen by God, he was loved by some but hated by others. He suffered undeserved rejection, with Saul plotting his death. He refused to take matters into his own hands, trusting the Lord to bring about his promises in his way and in his time. Even in times of extremity he proved himself by avoiding the faults of presumption, rashness, disobedience and infidelity that had marked out his predecessor.

MARK THESE WORDS

1. We have some more 'firsts' in this book: 'LORD of hosts' (1:3); 'Messiah' ('his anointed' 2:10); 'word of the LORD' (3:1); and 'Long live the king' (10:24).
2. Ring each 'he will take' in 8:10–22. Earth's kings take; God's King gives.
3. Ring each 'sheep' in 16:11–17:37 and notice David's care of the flock. Do we care as much for young Christians?
4. Ring each 'wisely' in chapter 18.
5. 'Despised and rejected', David was like Christ. What sort of people resorted to him at the cave of Adullam? See 22:1–2 and ring 3 words beginning with 'd' in verse 2. Which one are you like?
6. Study Samuel's prayer life: 7:5,8–9; 12:18–19,23; 15:11,35. Who was the other man known for prayer to God? See Jeremiah 15:1.

2 Samuel

Know the book

2 Samuel deals with the story of David—the king who was choice in God's sight (1 Samuel 13:14). It follows on from 1 Samuel, which dealt with Saul—the king who was choice in man's sight (1 Samuel 9:2).

David is the greatest of Israel's Old Testament kings. More space is devoted in the Bible to him than to any other person except Christ. Christ as Prophet is foreshadowed by Moses, Christ as Priest by Aaron, and Christ as King by David.

2 Samuel deals with how David came to the throne (seven years as king over Judah, before thirty-three years as king over all the nation of Israel). Then it recounts how he reigned on the throne, fled from the throne during his son Absalom's rebellion, and finally returned to the throne.

CH. 1–10 DAVID'S TRIUMPHS

CH. 11–12 DAVID'S SINS

CH. 13–24 DAVID'S TROUBLES

The early chapters of the book record the consolidation of the kingdom. David united it, made Jerusalem the theocratic centre, placed the ark there (symbolizing the presence of God) and made the kingdom secure by overcoming all enemies. Those factors have their parallels in Christ's kingdom as well.

In chapter 7, God makes an important covenant with David. Care must be taken to sort out the temporal and eternal promises. Some parts were fulfilled in David's son Solomon, but the covenant is also the beginning of a series of prophecies indicating that Christ would come 'of David'. By race Christ was 'of Adam'; by nation he was 'of Abraham'; by tribe he was 'of Judah'; by family he was 'of David'; and by specific birth he was 'of a virgin' (Isaiah 7:14).

The Bible is a book that shows the forgiveness of God, but it nowhere glosses over sin. 1 Samuel indicates that David resorted to lies and deceit on occasions. 2 Samuel shows his mistakes (for example, copying the pagan method in 6:3) and also his tragic sins (murder and adultery in ch. 11, pride in ch. 24). That such a saint should sin should teach us all not to presume; but where we have known failure of any sort, we should not despair.

The seven chapters which follow David's adultery and murder teach that, although there may be eternal remission of the penalty of sin, there is no earthly remission of consequences. When we have done with sin, sin has not done with us. The tragedies of Tamar and Amnon, and Absalom and civil war, all flowed from David's sin.

God's grace and power to overrule is shown in both of David's greatest sins. The son who built the temple, and the site where the temple was built, emerged from these tragedies.

2 Samuel 23:1 describes David as 'the sweet psalmist of Israel'. 2 Samuel 23:2 is a claim of divine inspiration; the psalms he wrote contain many prophecies of the coming Messiah, and were written during this period of history.

MARK THESE WORDS

1. In 11:1, ring 'sent'. Beware the first time 'went' becomes 'sent': those accustomed to serving the Lord must beware the temptation to stay at home and send others to take their place. Also ring 'but' in 11:1,27.
2. Psalm 51 is the sob of the saint—David's confession of sin. It is very personal. Ring each 'me' and 'my'.
3. In 13:1 ring 'after this', and notice that sin has consequences.
4. Look up the words ringed in Joshua 7:21. Did David follow the same course?
5. Underline Job 31:1. Such a covenant would have helped David. Are we disciplined and godly in what we look at and read?

1 Kings

Know the book

1 Kings and 2 Kings originally formed one book. They were only separated because of length difficulties in parchment copies.

The two books of Kings begin with King David and end with the king of Babylon; with the temple built, and then the temple burnt; with David's first successor, and then with his last successor. They start with glory—Solomon's; they end with shame—Jehoiachin's. They cover a period of over 400 years.

1 Kings is divided into two: the first eleven chapters deal with forty years of the united kingdom; the second eleven chapters deal with eighty years of the divided kingdom.

CH. 1–11 UNITED KINGDOM

CH. 12–22 DIVIDED KINGDOM

1 Kings commences with the death of David. After devoting so many chapters to his life, two verses suffice for his death, which only released his own soul for glory. By contrast, sixteen chapters are devoted to the death of Christ, which accomplished the redemption of millions.

Solomon succeeded David. He asked for wisdom to rule his people, but not wisdom to rule himself. His mind and his morals were not on the same level. He became the wisest fool who ever lived. Materially, his reign was of unparalleled success; spiritually, it was disastrous. His gradual apostasy achieved more damage than the infamous scandal of his father who sincerely repented. His three realms of sin were polygamy (many wives—though he only had one son recorded, and him a fool), polytheism (many gods) and pleasure (many indulgences). His greatest achievement was the building of the temple at Jerusalem. It was for the 'name of the LORD' (5:5). Solomon was too wise to think it was for God himself (8:27).

Jeroboam rebelled after Solomon's death to set up the northern kingdom, known as Israel—as opposed to the southern kingdom of Judah, where Rehoboam reigned as king. Jeroboam introduced new centres of worship, idols, a new altar, a new order of priests and a new annual feast. His tragic epitaph was 'he made Israel sin'. Fifteen of the succeeding eighteen kings of Israel follow this tragic example.

Elijah was the prophet to Israel to arrest the apostasy. He lived when Ahab ruled the land and Jezebel ruled Ahab. This wicked queen was the first person in the Bible to introduce national religious persecution. Like Luther and Knox, Elijah stood alone, calling the people back to the true God and his ways. He was a prophet of crisis, and Carmel was the apex of his ministry. The depression and flight which followed may have been brought on by loneliness and exhaustion. Let us beware these same two foes.

MARK THESE WORDS

1. 'As … David' is the commendable phrase to notice in the kings of Judah. Ring the words in 3:14; 9:4; 11:4,33,38; 14:8; 15:3,11. The Christian standard is 'as Christ' (1 John 2:6).
2. Underline 'Jeroboam … made Israel sin' in the second half of the book. How many times do the words occur? They also occur in 2 Kings.
3. Place the letters J (for Judah) or I (Israel), G (good) or B (bad), and a number by each king when he is first mentioned, so that I1B would stand for 'Israel's first king—bad'; J3G: 'Judah's third king—good'; etc.
4. Chapter 8 contains the longest prayer in the Bible. Read it out loud, and time yourself. Most Bible prayers are much briefer—remember to follow their example when in prayer meetings.
5. The hymn 'The Saviour has come in his mighty power' has the refrain, 'Oh, it is wonderful, it is marvellous and wonderful: What Jesus has done for this soul of mine, the half has never been told.' What story are the last words of this chorus based on?

2 Kings

Know the book

2 Kings continues the account of the divided kingdom started in 1 Kings. Although the title of the book draws attention to the kings, it is in fact the great prophetic period. Ahijah had prophesied against the dynasty of Jeroboam, which fell (1 Kings 15:29); Jehu had done the same with the line of Baasha which fell (1 Kings 16:12). 2 Kings contains similar prophetic fulfilments. The early chapters deal with the fall of the Ahab dynasty (10:10); the central chapters deal with the fall of the northern kingdom (17:23); while the concluding chapters cover the fall of the southern kingdom (24:2). 'Be sure your sin will find you out' (Numbers 32:23) is the clear emphasis, whether applied individually, to a family or to a nation.

CH. 1–10 LIFE OF ELISHA

CH. 11–17 FALL OF ISRAEL

CH. 18–25 FALL OF JUDAH

It should be remembered that Israel was taken into captivity by Assyria, and well over a century later, Judah by Babylon. In the Babylonian captivity there were three deportations: Daniel was taken in the first one and Ezekiel in the second, while Jeremiah was left in his homeland in the third.

2 Kings commences with the ministries of Elijah and Elisha. When God takes one workman to heaven (ch. 2) he still has another to carry on his work. Elisha received a 'double portion' (2:9). Whereas Elijah's miracles were mainly of judgement, Elisha's were mainly of grace. Elijah and Elisha can not only be contrasted with each other, but they can be compared with the contrasting ministries of John the Baptist and the Lord. See also Malachi 4:5, and compare it with Matthew 17:10–13. 'Elisha' means 'God saves', and is very similar to 'Je(hovah) shua' (Jesus), meaning 'the LORD saves'.

2 Kings 4 details the second of seven occasions when people were raised from the dead. The remaining six occasions were by Elijah (1 Kings 17:22),

the Lord (Luke 7:15; 8:55; John 11:44), Peter (Acts 9:40) and Paul (Acts 20:12).

It is interesting to note that, although there were many miracles in the northern kingdom, there were no revivals; while in the southern kingdom there were five revivals (see 2 Chronicles) but no miracles. The biblical record clusters miracles around four eras: the times of Moses, the prophets, Christ and the apostles.

2 Kings 5 details the story of Naaman. He needed healing from two diseases: pride and leprosy. Gehazi's faults were greed and deceit.

2 Kings 7 describes four lepers saved from starvation, whose logic should be adopted by every Christian: 'We are not doing right. This day is a day of good news, and we remain silent ... Now therefore, come, let us go and tell' (7:9).

MARK THESE WORDS

1. Continue to note each reference to 'Jeroboam ... made Israel sin' (as for 1 Kings).
2. Continue to place in your margin letters and numbers to show which king reigned where and when, and whether he was good or bad, e.g. I1B; J3G; etc.
3. Ring each 'man of God'—it appears 36 times.
4. Underline each 'he did evil (or 'what was right') in the sight of the LORD'. They occur 21 (8) times.
5. Ring each 'word of the LORD'—occurring 24 times.
6. Jezebel was the wicked queen of the north. Who was the wicked queen of the south? How were they related? How did the second one come to be in Judah?

1 Chronicles

Know the book

1 and 2 Chronicles repeat the history period dealt with in the books of Samuel and Kings. They do not contain mere repetition, however. Whereas the earlier books look at history from the human viewpoint, these look at the same period from the divine viewpoint. Samuel and Kings are concerned with political progress, while the books of Chronicles emphasize spiritual progress. Samuel and Kings show how man ruled history, and Chronicles shows how God overruled history. Christians should make sure their prayers do not reflect the world scene from the political viewpoint reported in the media, but should ask for wisdom to see how it relates to gospel progress or hindrance.

1 Chronicles covers the period from the creation of Adam to the death of David. It concentrates on the life of David, in particular the preliminary steps he took in paving the way for the construction of the temple in Jerusalem. These steps included bringing the Ark to Jerusalem (ch. 13–16), desiring to build the temple himself (ch. 17), obtaining the site for it (21:22) and preparing materials and organizing the ministry for it (ch. 23–29).

CH. 1–10 FOUNDATIONS OF THE NATION

CH. 11–29 PREPARATIONS FOR THE TEMPLE

The original title in the Hebrew Scriptures of the combined books of Chronicles was 'Omissions'. They include interesting extra details omitted in the earlier history books. 1 Chronicles informs us, for example, that God slew Saul (10:14), that Satan moved David to count the population (21:1), and that it was God who chose the site where the temple was to be built (21:18).

Items are also omitted which are included elsewhere: Saul's life is glossed over (ch. 10) as spiritually it was unimportant, and has nothing to contribute to the purpose of God, which is the main emphasis of the book.

David's fall into sin is also omitted. That serves to underline the fact that when God forgives, he forgets, for Chronicles was written more than 400 years after God had pardoned David's iniquity (see 2 Chronicles 36:23).

1 Chronicles starts with genealogies, or 'family trees'—but they are not 'endless genealogies'. They are recorded to emphasize that biblical faith is founded on definite historical fact. Moreover, there are some marvellous 'gems' to discover among the genealogies when reading through them. The prayer of Jabez (4:10) is still applicable for Christians to pray today: 'Oh (the deepest longing), that you (the highest source) would bless (the greatest privilege) me (the neediest person) indeed (the widest application).'

MARK THESE WORDS

1. History repeated in Chronicles is God's 'double knock'. Anything God says is important; when he repeats it, it is doubly important. How many people in the Bible can you list who had a personal double call? For starters, see Genesis 22:11; Exodus 3:4; 1 Samuel 3:10.

2. Ring 'with' and 'for' in 4:23, and muse on two wonderful blessings Christians have in the place where they live.

3. In chapter 12, which tribes 'joined David'? Were 'designated by name'? 'Had understanding of the times'? Were 'stouthearted'? Ring additional words describing David's mighty men that challenge Christians as to how they should serve the Lord. How well are you doing?

4. Memorize Hebrews 8:12 to remind you that when God forgives, he forgets.

2 Chronicles

Know the book

2 Chronicles continues to look at history from the divine viewpoint. In secular history all eyes are on what is happening at the palace of the kings. In spiritual history, the emphasis is on what is happening at the palace of the King of kings—namely, the temple.

2 Chronicles gives the history of what is known as Solomon's temple. In the opening chapters it is built; by the final chapter it is burnt. The concluding verses, however, hold out hope that a future temple would replace it—this was later built by Zerubbabel (see the book of Ezra).

The Bible teaches that there have been seven dwelling places on earth known as temples: those built by Moses (more frequently referred to as the tabernacle, but see 1 Samuel 3:3), Solomon, Zerubbabel and Herod; Christ himself (John 2:19–21); Christians collectively known as the 'church' or 'Christ's body' (Ephesians 2:21–22); and each Christian individually (1 Corinthians 6:19). It is clear from these that, whereas 'bricks and mortar' may have been the emphasis in the Old Testament, 'flesh and blood' is the emphasis in the New Testament. God does not live in buildings, but in his sin-washed people. What care Christians should take over body and mind, lest they become polluted temples of God (1 Corinthians 6:19–20).

2 Chronicles deals with the history of Judah—God's 'faithful' people—as opposed to Israel in the north—God's 'compromising or apostate' people. In spite of the latter being larger numerically, and having glorious statues and an extensively organized priesthood, the 'faithful' are constantly warned against joining with them. Because godly Jehoshaphat linked with the ungodly people of God, there resulted tragic marriage alliances, and the messianic line of promise was almost annihilated (ch. 22).

The book deals with the glory in Solomon's time, occasional 'glory' periods of reform, and concludes with the temple's glory gone.

CH. 1–9 PERIOD OF GLORY

CH. 10–35 PERIODIC GLORY

CH. 36 PASSING OF GLORY

There were five periods of reform or revival during the centuries of 'periodic glory':

(a) Asa (ch. 15)—mainly religious;

(b) Jehoshaphat (ch. 17)—mainly educational;

(c) Joash (ch. 24)—mainly ecclesiastical;

(d) Hezekiah (ch. 31)—mainly religious;

(e) Josiah (ch. 34)—mainly spiritual, but too little, too late.

2 Chronicles also includes further items omitted elsewhere. Of special note is the recorded conversion of Manasseh. He was the only bad king who became good late in life. Men may overlook 'deathbed conversions'— but God does not. Manasseh has been called 'the Old Testament prodigal', because he left his home of Jerusalem, but later returned to it (33:11–13).

Special instructions are given relative to the ministry of sacred music in 29:25–30. Instrumentalists and singers had to be from the dedicated Levites only. Wise, spiritual leaders advised on the choice of song after consulting the word of God (v. 25); not every instrument was acceptable (v. 27), and this particular revival turned them back to the old hymns of the past (v. 30).

MARK THESE WORDS

1. Ring each 'seek/sought the LORD' (20 times).
2. Ring each 'if' and 'when' in chapters 6 and 7.
3. Note the lovely definition of 'Amen' in 6:17.
4. 'He reigned ... and to no one's sorrow, departed.' Whose was this epitaph (see ch. 21)?

Ezra

Know the book

Ezra deals with the return of the Jews from Babylon. It is the story of another 'exodus'. Three times in their history the Jews have returned to their land:

(a) Under Moses, when redeemed from Egypt.

(b) With Zerubbabel, Ezra and Nehemiah, returning from the captivity in Babylon.

(c) In the 20th century, when they regathered from world dispersion.

Ezra is the first of three Old Testament history books that deal with the 'post-exilic' period. The other two are Esther and Nehemiah. They have the last three places in the seventeen history books. There were three 'post-exilic' prophets—Haggai, Zechariah and Malachi. They have the last three places in the seventeen prophetical books.

Ezra and Nehemiah are the two books which deal with the restoration of the Jews to the land of Israel. Esther is the book which deals with the preservation of the Jews for the land of Israel. In order of time, the book of Esther should be placed between chapters 6 and 7 of the book of Ezra.

Just as there were three stages in being deported into Babylon, so there were three stages in returning to Jerusalem:

(a) With Zerubbabel, who rebuilt the temple.

(b) With Ezra, who reformed the people.

(c) With Nehemiah, who reconstructed the walls of Jerusalem.

The book of Ezra deals with the first two stages, with about eighty years (and the history of Esther) between them.

CH. 1–6 REBUILDING THE TEMPLE

CH. 7–10 REFORMING THE PEOPLE

Ezra commences after the seventy years' captivity. Persia had replaced Babylon as world ruler. Cyrus (1:1) had been influenced by Daniel (Daniel 6:28). Zerubbabel had been born in Babylon (this was the meaning of his name), so he personally was not returning to Jerusalem, but setting out on his first visit. It was essentially a religious movement, as opposed to a political one. The altar was set up first (3:3), then the temple was started (3:10). After the work was begun (ch. 3), it was opposed (ch. 4), then resumed as a result of the challenges from Haggai and Zechariah (ch. 5), and eventually finished (ch. 6). They began at the centre, not at the edge. The heart must be sorted out first, before other matters in life are put right.

The second half of the book is about the man Ezra. The Jews called him the 'second Moses'. In 7:10 we see that he had determined to be a 'man of the Book'—he wanted to know it, obey it and teach it. It is believed that he wrote Chronicles, organized the sacred writings into the Old Testament canon, wrote Psalm 119, as well as Psalm 1 as a preface to the book of Psalms, and promoted the 'synagogue' as the local place to teach God's word.

MARK THESE WORDS

1. There are different descriptions for the Word of God. How many different ones are there in 1:1; 3:2; 6:14,18; 7:6,10,14; 9:4; 10:3,5?
2. Ring each 'the good hand of his God upon him' (or similar) in chapters 7–8 (six times).
3. Compare Ezra 10:1, Nehemiah 1:4 and Esther 8:3, and note that all three of them wept in their prayers.
4. How many written letters can you list in this book? Remember the power of the postman (don't forget those missionaries!).
5. 2 Timothy 2:15 aptly describes Ezra. Ring each 'ashamed' in 8:22 and 9:6. What was Ezra ashamed of? What can we safely deduce he was not ashamed of?

Nehemiah

Know the book

Nehemiah is the second of the three 'post-exilic' history books. Chronologically it is the last. It deals with the walls of Jerusalem being built. It concludes Old Testament history. The New Testament era commenced over 400 years later.

Nehemiah was an important Jewish official in the court of the Medes and Persians, when they were world rulers. Prayer and work formed a wonderful balance in his life and leadership.

Nehemiah began with prayer (1:4) when he prepared to ask for permission to return to build the walls of Jerusalem. He then continued in prayer throughout the project (4:9) and did not cease to pray, as is seen by the last verse in the book (13:31).

Nehemiah was also a model worker. Dr A. T. Pierson analysed his method as follows: (a) he introduced division of labour; (b) he adapted the work for the worker; (c) he promoted honesty and economy in administration; (d) he co-operated in labour; (e) he concentrated on any assaulted weak point.

He faced ridicule (4:3), anger (4:7), debris and depression (4:10), fear (4:14), greed (5:7) and craftiness (6:2). But he prayed on, built on and battled on—and was crowned with success.

CH. 1–7 REBUILDING THE WALLS

CH. 8–13 REFORMING THE PEOPLE

Nehemiah exhibited naturalness and dedication, both spiritually and practically. Every Christian should pray for similar qualities. The famous Methodist preacher Samuel Chadwick prayed: 'O Lord, make us intensely spiritual, but keep us perfectly natural, and thoroughly practical.' Although a good all-rounder, Nehemiah was given Ezra as a co-worker. The Bible makes quite clear, 'Two are better than one'. See Ecclesiastes 4:9–10.

Nehemiah shows Ezra to be the first scriptural preacher. He has been called 'the father of all our expository and experimental preachers'. Ezra 7:10 indicated that he had already invested time into becoming a 'man of the Book'. Nehemiah 8 now portrays him as a 'preacher of the Book'. In 8:4 we are told he used a 'platform … made for the purpose'. In 8:8 there is good advice for those who preach today: (a) read the Bible distinctly; (b) give the sense; (c) help people to understand what the passage means.

Chapters 8–10 contain a 'Back to the Bible' movement. The reading of the Word of God (ch. 8) is followed by prayer to God (ch. 9) and then resolve for God (ch. 10). That is a good order for each Quiet Time that a Christian has.

In 11:1 we read that leaders were living where they should, but others were willing to move to strengthen the cause of God. Are we?

Abusing the house of God, not paying the tithes of God, ignoring the Sabbath, and compromising in marriages, were four problems Nehemiah had to tackle in the final chapter. Old errors are ever reoccurring. Have we a clear conscience regarding this foursome?

MARK THESE WORDS

1. Prayers occur in 1:4–11; 2:4; 4:4–5; 5:19; 6:9,14; 13:14,22,29,31. How many of these are one-sentence prayers?
2. Ring the word 'work' each time (occuring 18 times). 'The work' they were doing was indeed 'a great work'—see 6:3.
3. The Word of God is referred to 43 times using 22 different phrases. How many different ones can you spot?
4. 'Tithes' are referred to five times. See Malachi 3:10, remembering that Malachi prophesied in the time of Nehemiah.
5. Ezra, driven to extremity, plucked off his own beard, but Nehemiah plucked off other people's! Find the references.

Esther

Know the book

Esther is the third of the three 'post-exilic' history books. The events it records occurred during the time interval between Ezra chapters 6 and 7. It is the wonderful story of the preservation of the Jews at a time when anti-Semitism threatened the survival of the nation. The elimination of the Jews may have been the desire of Haman the Agagite, but the elimination of the messianic line was the design of Satan. Haman did not want Mordecai to live. Satan did not want Jesus to be born.

The book of Esther nowhere uses the name 'God' directly. The reason may be that the book was written in the 'pagan' setting of the court of the empire of the Medes and Persians.

Esther is the Old Testament outworking of Romans 8:28. It is the 'Romance of Providence', or 'God working in the shadows'. Matthew Henry said, 'Though the name of God be not in it, the finger of God is.'

Esther records miracles of providential overruling rather than of supernatural intervention. Providence is a province where God rules; it is not fate, but is often consistent with responding to prayer and resolve. Esther chose to pray; Haman gambled on luck (3:7).

Esther was a Jewess. She became queen of the realm after the former queen had been deposed. She kept her racial identity secret until the Jews were threatened with elimination. She then used her influence with the king to deliver her people and safeguard the messianic line.

CH. 1–2 THE FEAST OF THE KING

CH. 3–7 THE FEAST OF THE QUEEN

CH. 8–10 THE FEAST OF THE JEWS

Chapter 1 refers to several laws of the Medes and Persians. Although they did not have the Bible as their guide, one of these rules was that nobody should feel compelled to drink wine, even if the function was a royal one. The chapter illustrates that drinking can cause indiscretion, domestic tension and divorce, and can even threaten the breakdown of life on a national scale.

Vashti was a queen who preferred to lose her crown of royalty rather than her crown of dignity. She said 'No' to something wrong, knowing that she risked her crown. Later in the book, Esther said 'Yes' to something right, knowing that she risked her life.

Haman, the enemy of the Jews, found that he was on the receiving end of the prayer in Psalm 35:7–8. 'He dug a pit, he dug it deep, he dug it for his brother; and for his sins, he tumbled in that pit dug for another.' Like Hitler of last century, he perished on the gallows of his own making.

Esther knew there was a time to fast, and a time to feast. The feast of Purim was ordained by the Jews (9:27) rather than by God. This implies that there is nothing wrong in God's people deciding to keep certain anniversaries reminding them of God's favour and blessing, even though there is no command to do so.

MARK THESE WORDS

1. Ring 'enemy of the Jews' in 3:10; 8:1; 9:10,24.
2. Find and ring 'a certain Jew … of Kish, a Benjamite'. Can you think of another Jew of the same ancestry who spared Agag in the first book of Samuel? (Remember Haman was an Agagite.)
3. Ring each 'Jew' and 'Jews' (over 40 times).
4. Underline the last 15 words of 4:14. Consider its application to your own life and witness in the place where you live.

Job

Know the book

Job is the first of the five poetical books. It deals with the problem of suffering. Prose is used in chapters 1 and 2 and in 42:7–17; poetry elsewhere.

Job is probably the oldest book in the Bible, written in the time of the patriarchs, or possibly before. It deals with one of the oldest problems in the world. Years ago, people did not really understand the problem of suffering. Today—it is much the same!

Job is the story of a righteous man who suffered the loss of his wealth, family and health. With his friends, he discusses the possible reasons for such calamities. Job did not find the answer to what he was asking, but by the end of the book he had lost his question. He realized that godly people have to trust where they cannot trace, knowing that 'Behind a frowning providence, God hides a smiling face' (William Cowper). Although the book takes the reader 'behind the scenes' to indicate some of the happenings in the heavenly realm, as far as Job was concerned, the reason for his suffering was sealed in the silence of God.

The visit of three unwise (even though intelligent) men is recorded in 2:11. Job called them 'miserable comforters' (16:2). They were the greatest help when they said nothing. They are an apt reminder for Christians not to sermonize when they go to anyone to sympathize.

The three cycles of speeches which make up most of the book show that they were philosophizing in the dark. When the Bible correctly reports spoken error, it does not mean that the Bible has lost its infallibility. Job thought God was unkind; his friends made the mistake of suggesting he was being punished for sin. These wrong ideas are faithfully recorded to show what a mess man gets into when he uses merely his own fallible reasoning.

In the end, Job proves to be the best comforter, because his trial and triumph have comforted thousands through the centuries.

CH. 1–2 THE TRIAL

CH. 3–41 DISCUSSING THE TRIAL

CH. 42 AFTER THE TRIAL

Job gives the lie to all those who argue today that if Christians are righteous, they will be both healthy and prosperous. Jesus was the most righteous person who ever lived, and yet he knew poverty and greater suffering than any man.

Job also gives the lie to those who maintain that, scientifically, the Bible is simplistic and unreliable. Dr A. T. Pierson said, 'There are more scientific hints in this book than in all the uninspired literature of the world up to the eighteenth century.' Examples of this can be seen in 38:13–14 and 26:7, which combine to teach that the earth is rotating in space.

Job, although the earliest Bible book to be written, has references to the return of Christ (19:25), the resurrection of the body (14:14–15 and 19:26–27) and the redemption of man (33:24–28).

MARK THESE WORDS

1. Underline the first verses of those chapters which contain the start of major speeches. How many such speeches are there?
2. Ring 'my opinion' (three times) in chapter 32. Elihu was honest—the other friends should have used the phrase as well, instead of dogmatizing.
3. Ring 'Satan' in chapters 1 and 2. Count the times.
4. Ring the personal pronouns 'I', 'me' and 'my' in chapter 29.
5. Ring each question mark in chapters 38 and 39. There was so much that Job did not know! He was gently being taught that he needed to trust God for the answers that eluded him—including the reason for his own suffering.

Psalms

Know the book

Psalms is the second of the five poetical books. It deals with the problem of prayer.

Psalms is both a hymn book and a prayer book. It can be used in private devotion or public worship. It shows the saint on his knees in every mood of life, amid conflicts and triumphs, burdens and blessings. Sometimes penitent, sometimes pleading, sometimes praising, he is nevertheless always praying. So should we be.

Psalms is often referred to as the 'Psalms of David'. He did not write all of them, but he wrote the majority. Expressing himself in the psalms was a greater achievement than establishing himself on the throne.

Psalms is at the centre of the Bible; it also contains the heart of the Bible. Martin Luther called it a 'Bible in miniature'.

Psalms is divided into five sections, or 'books' within the book. Each ends with a doxology. To some extent their contents parallel the emphases in the five books of Moses (the Pentateuch), dealing with man, redemption, the sanctuary, unrest in earth, and the Word of God.

Psalms 1–41 Book one
Psalms 42–72 Book two
Psalms 73–89 Book three
Psalms 90–106 Book four
Psalms 107–150 Book five

A brief additional psalm of David, not contained in this book, is given in 2 Samuel 23, where he claimed divine help to express them (see v. 2).

Hebrew poetry did not emphasize the rhyme and rhythm of our own style of poetry. It played on repetition of thought, or contrasts, or a pattern sequence of verses through the psalm. Be ready to spot the connection or contrast between the two halves of many of the verses.

Psalms 6, 25, 32, 38, 39, 40, 51, 102 and 130 are called the *penitential psalms*. They express deep sorrow for sins committed.

Psalms 2, 8, 16, 22, 45, 69, 72, 89, 110, 118 and 132 are called the *messianic psalms*. They preview the person and work of the Lord Jesus Christ.

Names are given to the various other types of psalms, but the best way of studying them is not to concentrate on their type, but to examine each one in turn, and discover its theme. It helps the concentration (and memory!) if you think of your own title for each one.

MARK THESE WORDS

1. Psalm 51 expresses personal sorrow for sin. Ring each 'I', 'me' and 'my'.
2. David has his own beatitudes. Ring 'blessed' in psalms 2:12; 33:12; 34:8; 84:4–5; 94:12; and 119:2. Four other psalms have the word 'blessed' in their first verses. Ring these extra 4.
3. The last 5 psalms are a 'Hallelujah Chorus'. They start and end with the words 'Praise the Lord!'. How many other psalms start in the same way?
4. Psalm 119 is an 'alphabetic psalm'—each set of 8 verses starts with a new letter of the Hebrew alphabet. Its theme is the Word of God. All but 4 verses describe it using one word or another. How many different descriptions does it contain?
5. Write by the side of the following psalms these suggested titles: Psalm 22: The crucified Saviour; Psalm 23: The caring Shepherd; Psalm 24: The coming Sovereign; Psalm 105: Blessings in history; and Psalm 106: Blots in history. Try to think up titles for others as well.

Proverbs

Know the book

Proverbs is the third of the five poetical books. It deals with the problem of right behaviour.

Proverbs, as the name suggests, is a collection of short, pithy sayings which teach moral and spiritual truths. It is a library of wisdom. Many proverbs are condensed parables. C. H. Spurgeon said, 'These three things go to the making of a proverb: shortness, sense and salt.'

Proverbs stresses duty, whereas Psalms emphasized devotion. In Job the saint is on his back; in Psalms the saint is on his knees; in Proverbs the saint is on his feet.

Proverbs contains laws of heaven for life on earth. It views the same subjects contained in the law through different eyes. The prophet would say that righteousness is just and correct; the philosopher would say that it is prudent. The prophet would say that sin is disobedience; the philosopher would say it is folly. Both are correct. This book views life through the eyes of the wise, rather than the spiritual, man. Solomon is the author of most of this book, although others contribute. The frequency of God's name in the book ('the LORD' occurs sixty-eight times) is an apt reminder that these proverbs are from heaven—they are not just secular maxims.

The first chapters are addressed to 'my son'—presumably the foolish Rehoboam; the middle chapters are mainly miscellaneous sayings; the final chapters contain grouped material by various authors.

> CH. 1–9 ADVICE FOR YOUNG MEN
> CH. 10–20 ADVICE FOR ALL MEN
> CH. 21–31 ADVICE FOR LEADERS

Proverbs can be studied in a variety of ways. Since it contains thirty-one chapters, it lends itself to a regular 'chapter a day for a month' system. Perhaps the best method of study, however, is to choose a topic and follow it through the book, since the book is like a tapestry, with many lines of thought interwoven throughout its chapters. Chapter 26 divides into three main subjects: 'The fool' (vv. 1–12), 'The lazy man' (vv. 13–16) and 'The tongue' (vv. 17–28). However, many individual verses elsewhere also deal with these three subjects.

Other subjects include: God and man; marriage and home; youth and old age; wealth and poverty; purity and impurity; truth and falsehood; soberness and drunkenness; diligence and laziness; time and eternity; etc.

The early chapters have much to say about the bad woman, with her temptations and wiles. The final chapter says much about the good woman, and her trustworthiness as a wife.

MARK THESE WORDS

1. Ring each 'my son' in chapters 1–7 (15 times).
2. Ring each 'wisdom' throughout the book.
3. Christ is typified by 'wisdom' in Proverbs. Read chapter 8 and consider it from the aspect of Christ speaking, rather than just an impersonal 'wisdom'.
4. A saying can be compared with another, an extension of another, or contrasted with another. The words 'Better … than …', '… And …' and '… But …' give the clues to these three different types of proverbs. Ring the different words in chapter 16 to find out what sort of proverbs are being used. (Many other chapters in the middle section could be dealt with the same way.)
5. Find a list of 'seven' in chapter 6, and 6 lists of 'four' in chapter 30.

Ecclesiastes

Know the book

Ecclesiastes is the fourth of the five poetical books. It deals with the problem of right values.

Ecclesiastes is a book which is so relevant today. It could spare people the bitterness of learning through personal experience, if only they would take notice of its message.

Ecclesiastes examines the question: 'Is there life before death?' Solomon was the author who probed this question. He had all the power, wealth, health, women and intelligence a man could wish for, yet found that satisfaction eluded him.

Ecclesiastes records the futile living and thinking of this Old Testament prodigal. It is the inspired confession of a failure. Only in the last chapter, like the prodigal son who turned his feet towards home, did he turn his thoughts towards God. A glimmer of light dawned at last. The book closes before dealing with the satisfaction that is to be found in the 'homecoming' to a saving God. Those exhilarating delights are contained in Solomon's other book, which is placed next in the biblical order.

Ecclesiastes traces Solomon's search for satisfaction in the realms of science (1:4–11), philosophy (1:12–18), pleasure (2:1–11), materialism (2:12–26), fatalism (3:1–15), deism (3:16–4:16), religion (5:1–7), wealth (5:8–6:12), and morality (ch. 7–12).

CH. 1–11 SEARCHING IN THE DARK

CH. 12 SENSING THE DAWN

One of Solomon's mistakes was that his search for happiness was earthbound. The key phrase is 'under the sun'. He also used repeatedly 'on the earth' and 'under heaven'. Until the final verses in the book, he never considered the realm 'above the sun'. For him, God was left out.

Another of his mistakes was that he was timebound. He had 'a time to be born, and a time to die' (3:2), but no reference to any time beyond the grave. For him, eternity was left out.

The book contains no 'the LORD said', yet God is speaking throughout. It shows how God overruled the backsliding of Solomon to bring us this inspired record which clearly teaches the futility of seeking for happiness, or even hopefulness, if God is ignored. Atheists and cultists regard Ecclesiastes as one of their favourite Bible books. They overlook its overall purpose, and quote random snippets of Solomon's melancholic reasoning to try to support their errors. But Solomon's words stand up to the test—kept in context, they nowhere teach the errors some claim.

Ecclesiastes is markedly different to other Bible books, however. Job teaches it is possible to have piety without prosperity, whereas Ecclesiastes teaches it is possible to have prosperity without piety. Psalms teaches it is possible for one of God's people to reach the heights of joy and praise; Ecclesiastes shows it is possible for one of God's people to backslide to the depths of morbidity and gloom.

The book concludes with a magnificent poem describing old age (12:1–8) and excellent advice for preachers (12:9–12).

MARK THESE WORDS

1. Ring each 'vanity' through the book. (It occurs 37 times.)
2. Ring each 'under the sun'. (It occurs 29 times.)
3. Backsliders talk too much about themselves (see Proverbs 14:14). Ring each 'I' in chapter 2, which demonstrates this point.
4. Underline the words in 7:2 which teach that it can be more instructive to attend a funeral than a festival.
5. Underline Jesus' words in John 4:13 which summarize this book.

The Song of Solomon

Know the book

The Song of Solomon is the fifth and final poetical book. It deals with the problem of love.

The Song of Solomon is one of the 1,005 songs that Solomon wrote (see 1 Kings 4:32). It is sometimes called 'The Song of Songs' because it is his best. Similar expressions are to be found in the Bible, such as 'Holy of holies' to describe the most holy place in the tabernacle, and 'King of kings' to describe the greatest king—the Lord Jesus Christ.

The Song of Solomon can be abbreviated to 'SOS', and it is a God-inspired 'SOS' to safeguard true love within the marriage bond. Marriage was ordained of God from creation (Genesis 2:21–25), it was sanctioned by Christ at Cana (John 2:1–11) and it is the analogy used to describe the final raptures in heaven of the saved at the marriage supper of the Lamb (Revelation 19:7–9).

The Song of Solomon is sometimes difficult to follow since the story changes from place to place, and speaker to speaker, without always indicating where the changes occur. The main characters are a Shulamite maiden and her shepherd-lover. A third person involved is a king who also seeks to win the maiden's affections. Some people think, however, that the king and the shepherd may be one and the same. The maiden, overwhelmed at being wooed by a king, is more easily wooed when he returns in the guise of a shepherd. Having thus won her affections, he returns later in royal splendour to claim his bride.

CH. 1–4 FIRST LOVE

CH. 5 FALTERING LOVE

CH. 6–8 FULLNESS OF LOVE

The Song of Solomon sanctions the intimacies within the marriage relationship. It promotes neither celibacy nor lust. Some of its expressions are such that Jewish leaders advised their young people not to read it before the age of thirty.

The Jews see in the book an analogy of God's love for his people Israel. They read it at Passover, which reminds them of the time when God delivered them from Egypt.

The Christian can see in it an analogy of Christ's love for his people—whether considered as the church, or as each individual soul, loved, wooed, won and washed from their sins in his blood. The book is therefore a parable, making divine things more difficult to see to those who do not love them, and plainer and more pleasant to those who do.

Ecclesiastes mournfully testified, 'I tried the broken cisterns, Lord, but ah, the waters failed! Even as I stooped to drink they fled, and mocked me as I wailed.' The Song of Solomon brings a far higher note: 'Now none but Christ can satisfy, none other Name for me! There's love and life and lasting joy, Lord Jesus, found in thee.' Ecclesiastes shows how poor a rich man may be; the Song of Solomon shows how rich a poor man may be.

The book emphasizes 'the beloved', 'he', 'his' and 'him'. To the Christian, the person of Christ is predominent throughout. All Christians should make sure that their prayer times contain thanksgiving (when we are taken up with our blessings), intercession (when we are taken up with our needs), and worship (when we should be taken up with him alone!).

MARK THESE WORDS
1. Ring each 'my beloved'—occurring 23 times.
2. The best key to this book is Psalm 45. Check your title for it.
3. Underline 2:7. Howard Guinness said such words should be written in letters of fire in every place where young people gather.

Isaiah

Know the book

Isaiah is the first of the five books known as the 'major prophets'. The authorship—questioned by some—is confirmed by Christ in John 12:37–41, where he quotes from early and later chapters of Isaiah (ch. 6 and 53).

Isaiah was a man who prophesied for about sixty years through the reigns of four kings, about 700 years before Christ. He was alongside good King Hezekiah of Judah at the time when the Assyrian Empire, having conquered the northern kingdom of Israel, were threatening to take the southern kingdom into captivity as well. Through the spiritual leadership and prayers of Hezekiah and Isaiah, they were spared conquest for over another hundred years.

Isaiah had influence in the palace. He was married with two children, and tradition maintains that he was put to death early in the reign of wicked Manasseh, by being sawn in two (see Hebrews 11:37).

Isaiah contains sixty-six chapters. They are like a miniature Bible, dividing into two main sections of thirty-nine and twenty-seven chapters, paralleling the number of books in the Old and New Testaments. The first section emphasizes *condemnation*, while the second section rejoices in the *comfort* of the Messiah's coming. The last twenty-seven chapters subdivide into three sections, nine chapters each, and all three conclude with a similar 'woe' pronounced on the wicked. See 48:22, 57:21 and 66:24.

CH. 1–35 PROPHETIC CONDEMNATION

CH. 36–39 HISTORIC COMMENT

CH. 40–66 PROPHETIC CONSOLATION

Isaiah also contains a book of burdens (ch. 13–23); book of songs (ch. 25–27), with extra songs of the vineyard (ch. 5), redeemer (ch. 12), blossoming desert (ch. 35) and restored life (ch. 54); and a book of woes (ch. 28–33).

Isaiah is the Hebrew name meaning 'salvation of Jehovah'. Isaiah has been called the 'evangelical prophet', or the 'fifth evangelist'. In his book, 'salvation' occurs twenty-eight times; 'save' occurs nineteen times; and 'saviour' occurs eight times.

His prophetic call is recorded in chapter 6; he preaches the cross in chapter 53; and he makes an evangelistic appeal in 55:6–7.

Of the final three sections of nine chapters each, the central section deals with the suffering Servant. The central chapter of that section deals with the smitten Saviour. The central verses in that chapter are 5–7, and bring us to the heart of what happened on the cross where the Saviour died. Note that Isaiah predicted this 700 years before Christ, but spoke of it in the past tense, for the slaying of the Lamb was 'foreordained before the foundation of the world' (1 Peter 1:20).

Not only did Isaiah's message save the people of his own time, but 45:22 was the verse that brought Spurgeon to Christ, and 53:5–6 was used to bring Calvin to Christ.

MARK THESE WORDS

1. Ring the 'I will's of Satan in 14:12–15.
2. Ring each 'Holy One of Israel' (it occurs 23 times).
3. Ring each 'woe' in chapters 5, 6, and 28–33.
4. Underline 58:13–14, which exhorts us to keep God's holy day.
5. Mark any verse you notice which deals with the life of the Lord, such as 7:14, 9:6 (his birth); 11:1 (his family); 11:2 (his anointing); 11:2,4 (his character); 42:1–4 (his gentleness); chapter 53 (his death); 25:8 (resurrection); etc.
6. Determine which things are 'everlasting' by looking them up and marking them in 24:5; 26:4; 33:14; 35:10; 40:28; 45:17; 51:11; 54:8; 55:3,13; 56:5; 60:19–20; 61:7–8; 63:12,16.

Jeremiah

Know the book

Jeremiah is the second of the five books of the 'major prophets'. Jeremiah was a man who prophesied for over forty years about 600 years before Christ. He was born in the reign of wicked King Manasseh, encouraged good King Josiah during the last revival in the southern kingdom of Judah, witnessed the destruction of Jerusalem, and, tradition maintains, he was stoned by his own people after he went into Egypt with the remnant fleeing from Judah.

Jeremiah was the prophet of Judah's midnight hour. He was a man of sympathy with a message of severity. A century before his ministry Isaiah had tried to save the nation from Assyria, and had succeeded. Jeremiah tried to save the nation from Babylon by advocating non-resistance, but he failed.

Jeremiah constantly urged backsliding Judah to return to God, otherwise they would suffer the consequences. His appeals were ignored, and wrath fell to the full, although God loved his people to the end. Individual backsliding also has a price to pay in a similar way.

'The word of the LORD' occurs over fifty times in this book. Some of the messages are dated, but there is no chronological order of them in the chapters.

CH. 1–38 BEFORE THE FALL

CH. 39 FALL OF JERUSALEM

CH. 40–52 AFTER THE FALL

Jeremiah was timid, and very sensitive. He pleaded he was too young to serve, when God called him (1:6). Mysteriously and wonderfully God knew him before conception (1:5). His distinct human personality did not depend on foetal development, which throws Bible light on the malpractice of current abortion.

Jeremiah has been called 'The weeping prophet', 'The prophet of the broken heart' and 'The prophet of the bleeding heart and iron will'.

Although there was no better patriot of his time, he was branded with the stigma of a traitor. He discovered that the enemies of a preacher can be those from his own town (11:19–21), family (12:6) and congregation (15:15–17), as well as general opposition (15:20). He was put in the stocks (20:2), thrown into a pit (38:6) and put in chains (40:1). He was forbidden to marry (16:2) because his sufferings were such that a gentle woman could not be asked to be his associate. Jeremiah was the Job among the prophets.

Jeremiah had to face false pastors (23:1–2), false prophets (23:9) and false priests (23:11). During his ministry the word of God was banned, burnt and constantly belittled.

The message of Jeremiah is relevant not only to the individual backslider, but doubly so to a nation caught up in apostasy and deep sin. Although God's heralds may be in a minority and constantly scorned, the rumblings of coming judgement will get louder by the minute until the inevitable falls.

MARK THESE WORDS

1. It would seem that all God's prophets were early risers (25:3–4). Ring the words which speak of early rising in 7:13,25; 11:7; 26:5; 29:19; 32:33; 35:14–15 and 44:4.
2. Ring each 'backsliding' (it occurs 13 times) and 'return' (47 times).
3. Write the word 'prayer' by 1:6; 4:10; 10:19–25; 12:1–4; 14:7–9,19–22; 15:15–18; 17:13–18; 18:19–23; 20:7; and 32:16–25.
4. Find out who were the two greatest men of prayer (15:1).
5. Ring each 'I will' of God in chapters 30–33.

Lamentations

Know the book

Lamentations was written by Jeremiah and is the third of the five books of the 'major prophets'.

Lamentations is the prophet's 'Song of sorrow' at the destruction of Jerusalem by the Babylonians. It is an elegy in a graveyard. Although the ruin of the city had proved that Jeremiah had been a true prophet, yet all he could do was weep. It was foreign to his nature to adopt an attitude of 'I told you so'.

Lamentations is a book of five chapters. Each chapter is an acrostic poem. Successive verses begin with the twenty-two letters of the Hebrew alphabet in order in chapters 1, 2, 3 (three each) and 4, and out of order in 5. Each chapter ends with a prayer, except chapter 4, which is followed by a whole chapter of prayer, chapter 5. An acrostic method was used to aid the memory, and is an apt reminder that God wants his people to hide his word in their hearts. See Psalm 119:11.

The central chapter is 3. At the heart of that chapter is verse 33. The margin rendering of this verse is 'God does not afflict from his heart'. When God chastens his people, he does not enjoy it.

CH. 1 THE PLIGHT OF THE CITY

CH. 2 THE ANGER OF THE LORD

CH. 3 THE GRIEF OF THE PROPHET

CH. 4 THE STATE OF THE PEOPLE

CH. 5 THE PRAYER OF THE REMNANT

Lamentations is read by Jews on the anniversary of the destruction of Jerusalem. Loyal Jews will chant or sing from this book every Friday at the Wailing Wall—the only surviving part of the temple, which has become a place of prayer for them.

There is a place in Jerusalem called 'Jeremiah's grotto', where, it is maintained, the prophet wept over the city. It is close to the claimed site of Golgotha. It would appear, therefore, that the suffering prophet wept in the place where the suffering Saviour died.

Years before Jeremiah, the prophet Jonah looked over the spared city of Nineveh, mindful that he had had 100 per cent success. Jeremiah could only look over the city of Jerusalem and contemplate 100 per cent failure. Years later, the Lord Jesus Christ wept over the same city. See Luke 19:41 and Matthew 23:37. Isaiah may have predicted the Saviour more than any other prophet, but Jeremiah prefigured the Saviour more than any other prophet.

MARK THESE WORDS

1. Underline the 'heart' of Lamentations in 3:33.
2. A number of verses have messianic application, such as 1:12; 2:15; 3:14–15; and 3:19–20. Underline these and any others that you think are applicable in the same way.
3. Charles Wesley's hymn starting 'All ye that pass by' uses wording from 1:12. The hymn is magnificent. See if you can look it up, and read it aloud slowly.
4. Underline 3:48–51. The prophet wept because of people in need. Do you? Are you using your prayer list regularly to pray for unsaved loved ones? If not, take time to make amends now.
5. Jeremiah prayed for a compassionate heart (see Jeremiah 9:1). Memorize the following words, and use them regularly as a prayer for personal compassion for others:

> Let me look at the crowd as my Saviour did
> Till my eyes with tears grow dim;
> Let me look till I pity the wandering sheep,
> And love them for love of him.

Ezekiel

Know the book

Ezekiel is the fourth book of the five 'major prophets'.

Ezekiel was born in the time of Josiah's revival, and lived in the same period as Jeremiah. At the age of twenty-five he was taken into captivity when Jerusalem was destroyed by the Babylonians. He became a preacher in a concentration camp at the age of thirty. He was a missionary to his own people. Like his New Testament equivalent John, who was a prisoner on the isle of Patmos, he saw heaven opened, visions of a man on the throne, and the glory of God. Those visions put both men on their faces.

Ezekiel was a prophet of visions, symbolic actions and allegories (like the meaningful stories in *Pilgrim's Progress*). His ministry brought much personal and painful suffering. For some time he was dumb (3:26; 24:27 and 33:22), lay on his side (4:4), lived on loathsome food (4:15), and his wife died, coinciding with the final demolishing of Jerusalem (24:16–18). Visions, symbolic actions and allegories can make for difficult reading, and young Jews were forbidden to read this book before they were thirty 'lest by the difficulties they met they should be prejudiced against the Scriptures.'

'Ichabod' means 'the glory has departed' (1 Samuel 4:21). That word seemed to summarize the Jerusalem situation. However, Ezekiel had a vision not only of glory departing, but also of glory returning. His prophecies interweave horror and hope.

CH. 1–3 HEAVENLY GLORY

CH. 4–24 DEPARTING GLORY

CH. 25–48 RETURNING GLORY

The book climaxes with an anticipation of a future city, and the final words gloriously proclaim 'THE LORD IS THERE' (48:35).

This book of glory is a book of the 'LORD God' (occurs over 200 times). It is a book of 'thus says the LORD' (120 times) and 'the word of the LORD came to me' (49 times). The word 'Spirit' occurs twenty-five times. Isaiah was the prophet of 'the Son', Jeremiah the prophet of 'the Father' and Ezekiel the prophet of 'the Spirit'.

Ezekiel 1 gives a vision of God. 'Likeness' occurs ten times, so a mental picture is not so important as a spiritual understanding here.

Ezekiel 3:18 and chapter 33 contain a vital message. People answer to God for their sins, but others have to answer for their souls if they neglect to warn them, and share the gospel.

Ezekiel 34 is the chapter of 'The bad shepherd' who does not seek, heal or feed the sheep. But God also promises here that he himself will come as 'The good shepherd' to do all these things (see John 10 and Psalm 23).

Ezekiel 37 is the vision of the valley of dry bones. Its main application is not resurrection from the dead, but of the Jews returning from exile (which has happened more than once).

MARK THESE WORDS

1. 'You shall know that I am the LORD.' The captivity cured once and for all the idolatry of the Jews. These words occur over 60 times in chapters 6–39. Ring each occurrence.
2. Note the 3 most righteous men in 14:14. Which one of them was still living in Ezekiel's time?
3. Underline the words which define 'repent' in 18:30.
4. What hints do we have of Satan's past in 28:11–19?
5. Ring each 'I will' spoken by God in chapter 34.
6. For a good start to a new year, have a good 'clean up' (see 45:18).

Daniel

Know the book

Daniel is the fifth and final book of the 'major prophets'. Daniel was only a teenager when he was deported to Babylon by Nebuchadnezzar among the first group of captives from Jerusalem. Shadrach, Meshach and Abednego were his friends and prayer partners (2:17–18). Together they became conscientious abstainers (ch. 1) and proved that purity pays. In chapter 3 the three friends would not bow (v. 12), budge (v. 18) or burn (v. 27), and proved that principle pays. Years later, as an old man, Daniel would not give up his Quiet Times (ch. 6) and proved that prayer pays. The book is full of these men taking courageous stands for God.

Daniel, like Joseph in Genesis, was raised from the status of a slave to help rule the land. He served in the courts of Babylon, then of the Medes and Persians. Jeremiah influenced the remnant at Jerusalem and Ezekiel the Jews in captivity, while Daniel influenced the kings in the palace. The first six chapters are mainly historical; the last six are mainly prophetical. The former contain the dreams of Nebuchadnezzar; the latter, the dreams of Daniel.

CH. 1–6 PERSONAL ADVENTURES

CH. 7–12 PERSONAL DREAMS

Daniel's name means 'God is judge'. The book is a judgement on worldly customs (ch. 1), wisdom (ch. 2), pride (ch. 3), impiety (ch. 4), persecution (ch. 6) and nations (ch. 7–12).

Daniel is 'The prophet of world history'. His book is the Old Testament equivalent of the New Testament book of Revelation. It gives a majestic sweep covering the centuries of Gentile world rule from his own time to its ultimate catastrophic end. The forgotten dream of the giant image in chapter 2 is the basic ABC to understanding world history.

Daniel also includes keys to interpretation (2:38 and 8:20). Where the Bible dogmatizes, we can be sure of the interpretation. Caution is needed otherwise.

Babylon, Medo-Persia, Greece and Rome have been the four world empires in history. The last named divided into two sections, east and west. In man's eyes they appeared as a giant colossus of a glorious man (ch. 2); in God's eyes they appear as beasts (ch. 7–8).

The speedy conquests of Greece under Alexander the Great (8:5) crushed the Medo-Persian empire (8:6–7). Thereafter, Greece subdivided into four (8:8), from one part of which emerged Antiochus Epiphanes (8:9), who opposed the Jews (8:11).

Daniel contains much prophecy which is now history. History is only prophecy fulfilled; prophecy is only history foretold. They combine to tell the same story, and are a constant reminder that 'God is still on the throne'.

MARK THESE WORDS

1. The purpose of Daniel is 'that the living may know that the Most High rules in the kingdom of men.' Underline these words in 4:17,25,32.
2. Ring each 'vision' or 'visions' (they occur over 30 times).
3. Daniel was the only Old Testament person described as being 'greatly beloved'. Ring the words in 9:23 and 10:11,19.
4. Note that 9:25–26 indicates the time of Christ's death (each prophetic day represents a year).
5. Note the praying in 2:18; 4:34; 6:10–11; 9:3–4,13,17,21; and 10:3,12. He who would be much *for* God should be much *with* God.
6. Underline 8:27. If you feel you don't understand prophecy, take heart—so did Daniel sometimes. Rise up, and do what he did!

Hosea

Know the book

Hosea is the first of the last twelve books in the Old Testament, which are called the 'minor prophets'. These prophets preached as much as the others, but they did not write as much. They are not 'minor' in value, only in bulk.

Hosea lived about 700 years before Christ. He was one of the final prophets to the northern kingdom of Israel. For two centuries the nation had followed the sin of Jeroboam, and had calf-centred worship in Dan and Bethel. Hosea prophesied during its last years before its collapse at the hands of the Assyrians. He was to the north what Jeremiah became to the south a century later. He was 'The prophet of Israel's decline and fall'.

Hosea started as a home missionary, about the same time that Jonah went as a foreign missionary to Nineveh. Hosea was partnered at home by the prophet Amos. Amos was stern, and emphasized righteousness. Hosea was tender and emphasized mercy. Between them they emphasized 'the goodness and severity of God' (Romans 11:22).

Hosea was commanded to marry an unfaithful woman, and realized that the national situation was mirrored in his own domestic life. The early chapters of his book deal with him as the faithful husband, and Gomer, his unfaithful wife. The latter part deals with Israel as the unfaithful nation, and God as the faithful Lord. Much has been written about the loyalty of a pure woman to an undeserving husband, but this book emphasizes it is possible for a strong man to be faithful to an undeserving wife.

CH. 1–3 DOMESTIC ILLUSTRATION

CH. 4–14 NATIONAL APPLICATION

Hosea exhibited something of the love of John, the tears of Jeremiah and the patience of Job as he tried to save his marriage.

Hosea turns to the language of uncleanness and whoredom to impart God's view of the nation's sin. Spiritual unfaithfulness is compared to sexual impurity—and God abhors both.

Hosea is the 'Book for backsliders'. There is one word used frequently in connection with Israel sinning and backsliding—the word 'Ephraim'. In this book it occurs thirty-seven times. The last chapter concludes with a final appeal from God for the nation to return from their backslidings. The prophet even includes a suggested prayer in 14:2–3, knowing that a child is sometimes lost for words when he or she wants to say 'sorry'.

The Lord is equally concerned when any of his children backslide individually. He is grieved when Christians leave their 'first love', and calls on them to return (see Revelation 2:4–5). It is at such times that it is good to have words suggested which could become a personal prayer. Perhaps none are more moving and helpful than those in the 'Sorry' psalm (Psalm 51).

MARK THESE WORDS

1. Ring each 'Ephraim' in the book.
2. Ring each 'return' in the book. (It occurs 15 times.)
3. In their backslidings Israel broke all of God's Ten Commandments (see Exodus 20). See if you can find verses in chapters 4, 5 and 6 which show this. A good start is 4:2, where several are mentioned.
4. In verses 4 and 5 of the final chapter, ring each 'I will' God promised. Then ring each resulting 'shall' in verses 5–8 (there are 7 altogether).
5. Consider your prayer list. Enter the name of someone who seems to be backsliding. Pray for this person, and visit or write to him or her.

Joel

Know the book

Joel is the second of the 'minor prophets'.

Joel means 'The Lord is God' or 'The Lord is my God'. There were fourteen lesser known people in the Old Testament with this name. They came from eight of the twelve tribes. God constantly has his people scattered through the land, even if most of them are not well known.

Joel the prophet was the son of Pethuel. Apart from that, we do not know anything about his background, his family, or where and when he lived. Suffice it to say that he served God in his generation in the place where he found himself. So should we.

Joel used local things to teach lasting things; the current events as a basis for reminding of coming events. He was an opportunist who turned the talking point of the day into an illustration which conveyed the burning message on his heart. We would do well to follow his example.

Joel found himself in a situation where a plague of locusts had ruined the crops and laid the countryside bare. Moses had taught that locusts and crop failure could be a means of divine chastisement (Deuteronomy 28:38–39). Solomon had been promised that prayer would bring respite from such disasters (1 Kings 8:37–40; 2 Chronicles 7:1). At such a time of national calamity, there is a place to call for national prayer and fasting. Joel was prepared to do so (1:14). So should we be.

Joel's prophecies, like so many more in the Old Testament, not only had a local application to the people of his own time, but they also contained much that had application for future years. Joel likened the suffering from the locust plague to a miniature dress rehearsal for more widespread judgement to come. Nevertheless, his words were intermingled with exhortations to return to the Lord (2:12), which could bring blessing (2:14). Joel warned, but avoided fatalism by pointing to a way out. So should we.

The countryside had been devastated, but God promised he would 'restore to [them] the years that the … locust has eaten' (2:25). A personal application of the book is to the Christian who has been going through a 'lean patch'. God's promise holds out the wonderful prospect of making up for wasted time. What a great consolation!

Joel has been called 'The prophet of the Holy Spirit'. His words in 2:28–32 were quoted by Peter in his sermon on the day of Pentecost (Acts 2:16–21), where they have a clear application to the blessing which flowed from Christ and his gospel.

Joel was an Old Testament Jew who realized that God's blessings were for both Jews and Gentiles. He was prepared to use the word 'whoever'. So should we be (2:32).

MARK THESE WORDS

1. One of the key phrases in the book is 'day of the LORD'. Ring each one in 1:15; 2:1,11,31 and 3:14.
2. Underline the first 14 words of 2:25, which contain such a wonderful promise to anyone going through a lean patch.
3. God does not want mere outward *signs* of sorrow, but inner *sighs* of sorrow as proof of repentance. Underline 2:13 and find the words in the 'Sorry' psalm (Psalm 51) which describe the 'rent heart'.
4. Have missionaries you know been having lean patches because you have not written to them? Try to make up for it.

Amos

Know the book

Amos is the third of the twelve 'minor prophets'.

Amos lived about 750 years before Christ, when the northern kingdom of Israel reached its zenith of power under Jeroboam II. Military strength had brought a period of material prosperity. Business was booming; affluence abounded; people were living in the lap of luxury. But economic prosperity is a breeding ground for spiritual poverty. Deuteronomy 6:10–13 warned against this. Israel was deaf to the warning. Are we?

Amos was not brought up in the colleges, but in the country. He was 'The farmer prophet' and used many agricultural illustrations. When God wants a worker, he invariably chooses a man who is busy. Moses and David looked after flocks, Elisha was a ploughman, Peter was a fisherman, William Carey cobbled shoes and Mary Slessor worked in a mill. They illustrate the truth of 1 Corinthians 1:26–29. Their only ordination was 'the mighty ordination of the nail-pierced hands'.

Amos means 'burden'. He was a worker burdened for the working classes. As the rich get richer, the poor often get poorer. Oppression of the poor is iniquitous in God's eyes. Amos lived in the south, but was a prophet to the north. Burdened people are always willing to move to the area of greater need. Are we?

Amos predicted coming calamity, in spite of the economic boom. Seven nations are first condemned (chapters 1 and 2) in a spiralling judgement working gradually closer to home. People tend to listen more if 'others' are condemned first. Predicted disaster came within four decades. These nations are really nowhere today.

CH. 1–9:10 GREED PUNISHED

CH. 9:11–15 GLORY PROMISED

Amos uses direct sermons (ch. 3–6) and visions or illustrations (ch. 7–9). Variation is often helpful to the preacher.

Amos found that when he witnessed, he was reported to the authorities

(7:10–11), told to shut up by the official religious leaders (7:12–13) and advised to return home and confine his preaching to the small circles who believed what he said. Unashamed of his background, he was not silenced, but clearly declared the commissioning he had received from God (7:14–15).

Amos had words against the women of the day (4:1). Men may have the power of leadership, but women have the power of influence. The moral standards of a nation never reach higher than the moral standards of its women. They can influence for good (Hannah, Lois and Eunice) or evil (Eve, Delilah and Jezebel). In a time of affluence and greed, Amos clearly drew attention to the contribution that women had had in promoting selfish greed and avarice.

MARK THESE WORDS

1. Ring each 'poor' in 2:6–7; 4:1; 5:11–12; and 8:4,6. Which of these verses best summarizes their ill-treatment which God hates?
2. 'For three transgressions … and for four'. Underline the 8 times in chapters 1 and 2 that this expression occurs. God is patient about sin, but it is possible to do it once too often.
3. Three chapters contain sermons. They start with 'Hear this'. Underline the three occasions.
4. In chapter 4 there are 5 occurrences of '"Yet you have not returned to me," says the LORD.' Underline them, and the consequence: 'Therefore … prepare to meet your God.' By repenting we meet God in mercy; by refusing we meet God in judgement.
5. Who and what are we to 'seek'? Ring each occasion the word occurs in chapter 5 (four times) and chapter 8 (once).

Obadiah

Know the book

Obadiah is the fourth of the twelve 'minor prophets'.

Obadiah means 'Servant of the LORD'. The Bible refers to twelve other men with the same name. Little is known about any of them. God's true servants always speak little of themselves. The message is more important than the messenger.

Obadiah is a small book but deals with the biggest sin—pride. The age of the book is unknown, but the sin is the oldest of all sins. It turned an angel into a devil (Isaiah 14:12–15), depopulated heaven (Revelation 12:9), emptied Eden (Genesis 3:23), caused Christ to die, keeps hearts closed to his salvation and thereby populates hell. It is a sin that is even found in the small (Obadiah v. 2).

Obadiah is the 'Prophet of unbrotherly conduct'. If the first sin was pride, the first murder was that of a brother (Genesis 4). The book deals with the family feud traced back to Jacob and Esau (Genesis 25,27, etc.). Their descendants were known as the children of Israel and Edom. The Edomites could not forget, and would not forgive, family differences of bygone times. They refused to help when Moses requested passage through their territory, as the Israelites journeyed to the Promised Land; they did not grieve whenever the Israelites got into difficulties. Instead they gloated over their setbacks, looted their property and betrayed them into the hands of their enemies. They prided themselves in what they thought was an invincible mountain fortress of Petra (v. 3). But Obadiah's words were to come true. They were to become a nation reduced to nothing. The last Edomites were the Herods in the time of Christ. They maintained cruel treatment of the Jews to the end. Christ had nothing to say to the Herod he was taunted by (Luke 23:8–9). Today, the nation does not exist.

Vv. 1–16 The ill-treater doomed
Vv. 17–21 The ill-treated delivered

Obadiah was also a prophet of poetic justice. He clearly taught 'as you have done, it shall be done to you' (v. 15). Haman was hanged on his own gallows; the cruel Assyrians crushed by Babylon; then Babylon was crushed by Persia, Persia by Greece, Greece by Rome, Rome by the Barbarians ... 'So shall all the nations drink continually ... They shall be as though they had never been' (v. 16).

Obadiah has a personal application for the Christian. Christians are to 'love as brothers' (1 Peter 3:8). There must be no place for bitterness, resentment or jealousy. We are not to become 'silent spectators' when our brothers fall into difficulties. We are not to glory in their decline. Do you know a Christian who has fallen into sin or some difficulty? Do you know a neighbouring church declining in numbers, whose very existence is threatened? Do you know a denomination which has drifted from its first glorious faithfulness to Christ and the gospel? Do not be seduced into sinful smugness, or any sense of satisfaction or superiority. Weep for them. Pray—and if possible, extend the helpful brotherly hand.

Obadiah has a further application to all nations who oppose the Jews. The sin of anti-Semitism is very old. See Genesis 12:3 and Numbers 24:9 for God's special promises linked with people's different attitudes to the Jews.

MARK THESE WORDS

1. Note verse 4. Name one who is also described like this (see Isaiah 14).
2. Name one who humbled himself and was exalted (see Philippians 2).
3. Ring the phrase of 6 words which occurs 3 times in verse 13.
4. Eight Edomite mistakes are in verses 12–14. Pray that you avoid the 3 in verse 12 when you see another Christian in difficulties.
5. 1 Peter 3:8 states 5 things Christians should be. How many of these did the Edomites fail to achieve? How about you?

Jonah

Know the book

Jonah is the fifth of the twelve 'minor prophets'.

Jonah does not contain a made-up story, but is historical fact. The Lord Jesus endorsed it in Matthew 12:39–41. Its main subject is not of a man being swallowed by a whale, but of a God being interested in foreign missions.

Jonah was a prophet who lived in the northern kingdom of Israel about 750 years before Christ. His ministry was a little while after Elisha's, and just before those of Amos and Hosea. The arch-enemy threatening his nation at the time was Assyria whose capital city, Nineveh, was 500 miles north-east of Israel.

Jonah was commissioned to go to preach in Nineveh, urging repentance lest the city should be destroyed. Possibly out of a false patriotism, he became a reluctant missionary who sailed west to avoid the task. His name means 'dove', but instead of being a messenger of peace, he flew away from his responsibility.

Jonah discovered that God used many aspects of nature, including a whale, to get him back on course. Eventually, Jonah preached at Nineveh, and the city repented and was spared. Both Jonah and Nineveh were given second chances. God is often the God of a second chance—he gave it to Moses, Samson, Elijah, Peter and others after times of failure, defeat, depression and denial. 'Let's start again' must be part of his tenderest vocabulary.

CH. 1 THE PRODIGAL PROPHET

CH. 2 THE PRAYING PROPHET

CH. 3 THE PREACHING PROPHET

CH. 4 THE POUTING PROPHET

Jonah was not only slow to serve, he was also sullen in success. He had to learn 'There's a wideness in God's mercy …' Jonah was taught a lesson about God's love by a plant outside a city wall (4:5–10). The Christian is taught a lesson about God's love by a tree outside a city wall (the cross on Calvary, outside Jerusalem). About 800 years after Jonah left Joppa (1:3), Peter ('the son of Jonah', John 21:15) left the same city (Acts 10:5,23) to start Christian missionary work among the Gentiles. He had learnt that God loves the 'whoever' (Acts 10:43).

Jonah also contains a prophetic picture within its unfolding story. Jonah's experience with the whale typified Christ who was sent, suffered, buried for three days and nights, and rose to offer salvation to the Gentiles. This is declared in Matthew 12:39–41.

MARK THESE WORDS

1. Esther showed God's control of *providence*; Jonah shows God's control of *nature*. He sent a storm (1:4) and on four occasions 'prepared' other things. Ring the word each time and note what he used to bring about blessing.
2. The path of disobedience is always 'down'. Ring this word (it occurs 4 times in ch. 1 and once in ch. 2).
3. The word 'great' occurs in connection with four different things in chapter 1, but look up 4:2 to discover something which is greater than them all.
4. Ring each 'but' in 1:3 and 4:1. The first 'but' describes a disobedient action; the second a displeased attitude. God successfully overcame Jonah's disobedience. Sadly, there is no record that Jonah's attitude was changed. Search your heart, and make sure there is no lurking resentment about the salvation of somebody you don't like. If so, seek cleansing, and ask for a compassionate heart in tune with the Saviour's.

Micah

Know the book

Micah is the sixth of the twelve 'minor prophets'.

Micah lived about 700 years before Christ, when the Assyrians were about to defeat the northern kingdom of Israel, and threaten the southern kingdom of Judah. He was a contemporary of Isaiah. Isaiah was God's messenger in the palace; Micah was God's messenger to the people. Isaiah dealt with political matters; Micah dealt with personal matters.

Micah contains three prophecies against nations, leaders and people. Each begins with 'Hear'. Each section, however, concludes with words of 'cheer' (2:12–13; 5:7–15; and 7:18–20). Because of this he has been called a prophet of 'doom and glory'.

CH. 1–2 NATIONAL FAULTS

CH. 3–5 LEADERSHIP FAULTS

CH. 6–7 INDIVIDUAL FAULTS

Micah first dealt with the sins of the nations. Samaria and Jerusalem (1:5) were the capitals of Israel and Judah. The heart of the problem is always at the heart, whether nationally or individually. Micah is another prophet who condemns the oppression of the poor (2:2), defends the rights of women and children (2:9) and is included among the honoured brigade who are told to shut up (2:6).

Micah next dealt with the sins of the leaders. Princes, priests and prophets had all become mercenary and materialistic (3:11). God's servants must avoid the pitfalls of fear, fame and fortune. Money must not be allowed to buy mouths—either by silencing the messenger completely, or softening his message by compromise.

Micah was not concerned about the lining of his pocket; he was concerned about the anointing of the Spirit (3:8).

Micah then dealt with the sins of the people. His 'golden rule' (6:8) summarized man's need to be considerate, compassionate and contrite. He should live as a man among men (justly), adopting God's attitude among men (loving mercy), and living correctly as a man with God (walking humbly). Matthew 23:23 refers to these three, but equates the third with 'faith'. Micah 6:8 shows that God requires things of man, and reveals things to man. Micah 4:10 says that he also redeems man. This strong emphasis on correct all-round behaviour means that Micah was a 'Prophet of practical religion'.

Micah also prophesied of Christ. Whereas Isaiah said much about Christ's death, it was Micah who spoke about his birth. The 'everlasting' Lord would have a Bethlehem birth, en route to a royal throne (5:2). There is also a reference to his suffering, indicating that he would be struck (5:1).

MARK THESE WORDS

1. Ring each 'hear' in 1:2; 3:1; and 6:1.
2. Underline 6:8.
3. Compare 3:8 with Zechariah 4:6 and Acts 1:8. Who is the source of power in all witnessing?
4. Micah means 'Who is like the LORD?' He concluded his book with a magnificent poem in 7:18–20. Can you list 10 wonderful things God does, according to this section? There certainly is nobody else like him!
5. The chorus of the hymn 'Great God of wonders' by Samuel Davies is based on a verse in Micah. Look up the hymn, read the chorus, then find the verse in the last chapter of Micah.

Nahum

Know the book

Nahum is the seventh of the twelve 'minor prophets'.

Nahum was the second of the 'minor prophets' whose ministry was confined to the Gentiles. About 150 years before his time, Jonah had been sent to Nineveh to preach that the city should repent. Nahum prophesied against the same city, because it had repented of its repentance, and had turned to its cruel, oppressive ways again.

Jonah's message had been: 'Now is the accepted time!' Nahum's message was: 'Now it is too late!'

Jonah had revealed that God was the God of the second chance. Nahum revealed that God was the God of the final word.

Between them, these two prophets underlined the truth of Romans 11:22: 'Therefore consider the goodness and severity of God.'

Nahum prophesied against Nineveh when it dominated the world. The city had 1,200 towers, each 200 feet high. Its walls were 100 feet high, 60 miles in circumference, and so thick that three chariots could be driven abreast on them. It was vast; it was also vile (1:14). It is tragic when either nations or individuals become so bad that the best thing is for God to bury them. God dug a grave for Nineveh so well that every trace disappeared, and for centuries not even the site of it was known. God may be slow to anger (1:3), and he can forgive sin, but he is also angry with and punishes persistent sin. The Assyrians had been warned by Jonah, and had received mercy. To sin after that was to sin against both light and love. Twice in the book of Nahum, God said to them, 'I am against you.' Within fifty years the city was destroyed by the Babylonians. They experienced the outworking of God's earlier decree: 'My Spirit shall not strive with man for ever' (Genesis 6:3). Their epitaph is: 'It is a fearful thing to fall into the hands of the living God' (Hebrews 10:31).

Nahum means 'Comfort'. There is no comfort in the book for the ungodly, for it sounds their 'death song'. Nevertheless, there is comfort for the godly. The book demonstrates that God responds to humanity's cry for justice.

Capernaum means 'City of Nahum'. It is interesting to note that the Saviour commenced his ministry from this 'City of Comfort' (Matthew 4:13).

God is the God of all grace, and the Bible is a book of such blessing, but God has seen fit to include this solemn book of Nahum within Scripture. There is a place to announce the awful doom of the apostate, and the final judgement on those who persevere in their sins.

MARK THESE WORDS

1. Underline the first half of 1:3.
2. Note that in 1:2 'the LORD avenges' is emphasized 3 times. Threefold repetition occurs elsewhere in the Bible, and underlines the truth that the triune God (Father, Son and Holy Spirit) is behind the action.
3. We sometimes refer to the 'wrath' of God. Ring the three different words in 1:6 which are used for this.
4. Find the two occasions in the book where God says, 'I am against you.' Ring the words. Then underline the magnificent words the Christian can rejoice in—the second half of Romans 8:31.

Habakkuk

Know the book

Habakkuk is the eighth of the twelve 'minor prophets'.

Habakkuk was the last 'minor prophet' to Judah before that country collapsed beneath the Babylonian conquest, approximately 600 years before Christ.

Habakkuk was 'The questioning prophet' who did not understand why God could punish one ungodly nation (Judah) by using an even more ungodly nation (Babylon—see 1:13). The question still perplexes people in our own time. Job struggled to find the reason for personal suffering; Habakkuk struggled to find the reason for national suffering. Esther teaches that God is a God of providence. Habakkuk also teaches that God is a God of providence—even if that providence is perplexing!

Habakkuk found that the best place to speak about his secret thoughts was in secret. He poured out his difficulties to God in prayer, and waited patiently for an answer (2:1). He had been grieved by man's sin (1:3–4) and was troubled by God's initial silence (1:2). But God's answers came. Habakkuk learnt that all nations must answer for their sins, and in any war that includes both the loser and the victor. Obadiah had prophesied the end of Edom; Nahum the end of Assyria, and Habakkuk revealed the ultimate end of Babylon. The three nations no longer exist. They lie buried in long-forgotten graves.

The first chapter deals with the burden which worried Habakkuk; the second deals with the vision that reassured him; the third concludes the book with his prayer and final burst of song.

CH. 1–2 OUTWARDLY CONFUSED

CH. 3 INWARDLY CONTENT

The book is a mixture of Habakkuk speaking to God on behalf of men, and him speaking to men on behalf of God. Every servant of God should be engaged in both ministries. Are you?

Habakkuk has been called 'The grandfather of the Reformation'. It is in

2:4 that the Bible first says, 'The just shall live by ... faith.' Paul proclaimed that truth in the New Testament, and centuries later it was to transform Martin Luther.

Habakkuk's prayer is: 'Revive your work in the midst of the years' (3:2). Christians may anticipate the near return of the Lord Jesus, but their constant prayer should not only be for that coming (Revelation 22:20), but also for God's work to be revived in the intervening years. Christ's return is the hope of the church, but will bring disaster to millions of unsaved. Such people need to come to Christ, so their hope is not in the return of Christ, but rather in the revival of his work.

Habakkuk concludes with a song of joyful invincibility (3:17–19). In spite of adverse circumstances he was determined to rejoice 'in God my Jesus' (as Augustine translated it). The Christian source of joy is in the Blesser—not the blessings. Circumstances may cause outward perplexity and confusion, but should never be allowed to rob any Christian of inward contentment.

MARK THESE WORDS

1. In chapter 1 ring the verse numbers if they contain prayer by Habakkuk.
2. In chapter 2 ring the five occurrences of 'woe', and decide which sin is being condemned each time.
3. The Reformation 'verse' is in 2:4, and can also be found in Romans 1, Galatians 3 and Hebrews 10. Underline the four occasions.
4. Habakkuk prayed for revival. Are you up to date with your prayer diary for unconverted friends, as well as interceding for missionaries you know? Make 3:2 your own prayer now.

Zephaniah

Know the book

Zephaniah is the ninth of the twelve 'minor prophets'.

Zephaniah means 'Hidden of Jehovah'. He was born during the wicked reign of Manasseh, king of Judah. He was of royal blood (1:1), and like Moses and Joash before him, may have required protection in his early years. He survived, however, and his name became part of his message (2:3). The southern kingdom of Judah was within three decades of being conquered by the Babylonians. Zephaniah reassured the people that a godly remnant would survive—'hidden in the day of the LORD's anger' (see Psalm 32:6–7).

Zephaniah prophesied in the reign of Josiah, and may well have been responsible for the last period of Judah's revivals under that king. Corruption was widespread and deep rooted. The reforms therefore achieved too little, too late. Many of them were only superficial improvements. Princes were still cruel, judges still bought by bribes, prophets still shared only what the people wanted to hear, and the priests were still unclean (3:3–4).

Zephaniah spoke much about the coming 'day' of judgement. He used a good deal of 'hellfire' preaching. His motive was not to frighten people out of their wits, but to frighten them out of their sins (2:1–3). Nahum preached judgement as a deserved end in itself; Zephaniah preached judgement as a means of purification.

The first chapter deals with the judgement of Judah; the second deals with the judgement of surrounding nations; the final one concludes the book with promises for the distant future, and a triumphant song of joy. The first two chapters emphasize people sinking beneath God's heavy hand upon them; the last chapter concludes with people singing because of God's gracious hand beneath them. The opening verses 'I will consume ... I will cut off' (1:3) are in marked contrast to the 'I will bring you back ... I will give you fame and praise' of the final verse.

Habakkuk concludes with the prophet singing; Zephaniah concludes by encouraging the people to sing (3:14), and by declaring that God sings over them (3:17).

Whenever God rejects man, it is because man has rejected God. In 1:5–6 are four different principles of rejection. Applied to our day, they describe the following people:

(a) Those who do not want Christ, but something else.

(b) Those who want not only Christ, but something else.

(c) Those who once followed Christ, but now something else.

(d) Those who know they should follow Christ, but do not seek him.

The Christian should say, 'For me, Christ; Christ only; Christ always, and Christ wholeheartedly.'

MARK THESE WORDS

1. Ring each 'day' (it occurs at least 20 times). Note that each is in the context of judgement, i.e. 'day of the Lord'.

2. Ring each 'I will' in chapter 1, and note the contrast with each 'I will' or 'He will' of 3:14–20. Ring these also.

3. In chapter 2, one main word occurs twice in verse 1, another word three times in verse 3. Ring them. Do they suggest a good reason for attending Christian meetings?

4. Underline the 3 things we are to take positive steps to search for, as given in 2:3.

5. Ring each 'midst' in chapter 3. Who or what is central in the last of these?

Haggai

Know the book

Haggai is the tenth of the twelve 'minor prophets'.

Haggai, Zechariah and Malachi are called 'post-exilic' prophets because they prophesied after the Jewish remnant returned from the Babylonian exile or captivity. Their books are placed as the last three in the Old Testament. Their period of ministry was roughly between 500 and 400 years before Christ.

Haggai and Zechariah both prophesied in the time shortly after Zerubbabel returned to Jerusalem to rebuild the temple. Haggai was the realist; Zechariah was the visionary. Haggai's recorded ministry was for a period of three months; Zechariah's was for three years. God uses different men, in different ways, for varying periods of time. Short or long—let us serve well.

Haggai was the prophet who did not fight against corruption or compromise so much as against complacency. The rebuilding of the temple had commenced, but had not been completed. The people had been sidetracked. They were concentrating on building their own homes and feathering their own nests, at the cost of neglecting God's work. Similar things can still happen today. Haggai's whirlwind ministry rebuked sloth, called to self-examination with a thundering 'Consider your ways', and insisted on first things first. He was 'The prophet of priorities'.

He rebuked the 'time has not come' procrastinators. The question of whether it is the right time to serve the Lord still has very few replying 'No'—more say 'Not yet'—while God says, 'Now is the accepted time!' To wait for a time which is convenient for self and others, one might just as well wait for a time which is convenient for the devil—such a time would never come.

Haggai explained that great efforts (1:6) and high hopes (1:9) had only brought discouraging disappointment because priorities were wrong (1:9). Half-hearted obedience never results in God's wholehearted blessing.

Haggai not only preached, he also worked (Ezra 5:1–2). Later messages brought encouragement (1:13 and 2:4), promise of blessing (2:19), and reminders of God's approval and reward (2:23). He was a prophet who balanced criticism with commendation. There was more of the latter than the former. He may have stung them into initial action, but he solaced them thereafter. Within the amazing brief period of three months, the work was completed.

CH. 1 THE UNFINISHED WORK

CH. 2 THE FINISHED WORK

MARK THESE WORDS

1. Ring 'Consider your ways!' in 1:5, 7. A similar expression occurs in chapter 2. What is to be considered there?
2. Ring each 'the word of the LORD'. How many messages does Haggai give? (Most of his sermons are dated, but don't overlook 1:13.)
3. Note 1:13. It is important for each messenger of the Lord to have the Lord's message for the appropriate occasion.
4. Underline 2:19. For the Christian, 'The best is yet to be!'
5. 'Consider your ways!' What are your priorities? How are your Quiet Times? Prayers? Letters? Visiting? Care of others? Is your dedication to Christ beginning to take a lower place?

> Facing a task unfinished,
> That drives us to our knees,
> A need that, undiminished,
> Rebukes our slothful ease,
> We, who rejoice to know thee,
> Renew before thy throne
> The solemn pledge we owe thee
> To go and make thee known   (Frank Houghton).

Pray today that you may be helped to keep first things first.

Zechariah

Know the book

Zechariah is the eleventh of the twelve 'minor prophets'. He was a contemporary of Haggai. Their ministry was to encourage a despondent, relatively small group of Jews who had returned from exile about 500 years before Christ.

Zechariah means 'Remembered by Jehovah'. His father's name was Berechiah, which means 'Blessed by Jehovah'. His family upbringing would seem to have been a godly one. That is in marked contrast to what he says about fathers in 1:1–6.

Zechariah is a book containing many visions in the first six chapters; messages in the next two chapters, and two 'burdens' (see 9:1 and 12:1) in the last six chapters. The early section was more immediately relevant to the current situation in Zechariah's time; the third section contains many references to Christ and his Kingdom.

CH. 1–8 CONCERNING THE JEWS

CH. 9–14 CONCERNING THE KING OF THE JEWS

It is difficult to understand the meaning of some Bible 'visions'. If we cannot master Zechariah's, at least let us master lessons from the attitude he adopted. He was willing to admit his ignorance, ask questions, and was ready to learn where he could and leave alone where he couldn't. When asked, 'Do you understand?' he was not afraid to say 'No' (see 1:9,19,21; 4:4–5,11–13; 5:6,10; etc.).

As Christians we must remind ourselves that our faith is based on definite historical fact and the clear promises of God. It does not rest on the disputed interpretations of difficult visions. It is worth recalling the effect of a vision on Daniel (Daniel 8:27) and remembering the wise steps he took thereafter, which are an excellent example for us to follow.

Zechariah contains more messianic prophecies than any other Old Testament book apart from Isaiah. Zechariah focuses on the two comings of Christ (one now fulfilled, and the second still in the future). For this reason he has been referred to as 'The prophet of the advents'. Here are some verses which relate to various aspects of the life of Christ:

(a) 2:10–11: Coming to live 'in the midst' of his people.

(b) 3:8: 'The BRANCH' will be God's Servant.

(c) 6:12–13: 'The BRANCH' will be a Man, and a Priest-King.

(d) 9:9: The Saviour-King riding on a donkey.

(e) 11:13: Priced at thirty pieces of silver.

(f) 12:10: Pierced.

(g) 13:6: Wounded in hands by friends (see margin note).

(h) 13:7: God's co-equal: the Shepherd struck by God.

(i) 14:4: Yet to stand on a split Mount of Olives.

(j) 14:5: Yet to come, with all the saints with him.

MARK THESE WORDS

1. Ring every 'LORD of hosts' (it occurs over 50 times).
2. Ring 'fathers' in 1:1–6. There are some fathers we should not be like. What sort are they?
3. Ring 'the word of the LORD came' in chapters 7 and 8. The words mark the messages which Zechariah gave.
4. Ring each 'I will' of God in 10:6–12.
5. Go carefully through the book, ringing the number of each verse where you notice a messianic prophecy (such as the ones listed above). For additional blessing, write them out in the order in which they occurred in the life of Christ. Then sit back, read them, and marvel at how much of the biography of the Saviour was written in this book 500 years before he actually came.

Malachi

Know the book

Malachi is the last of the twelve 'minor prophets'.

Malachi means 'Messenger'. Malachi was not just any messenger, he was the last messenger of the Old Testament. His was the last book of Scripture to be written before the coming of Christ. His death was followed by 400 years of prophetic silence. That silence was broken when Christ came.

Malachi lived during the same period as Nehemiah. They opposed the same sins of the day (see Nehemiah 13). Idolatry had been cured during the captivity, but heart-backsliding was still rampant.

The book opens by declaring God's love for his people (1:2). The Hebrew literally means, 'I have loved you, do love you and will continue to love you.' Yet it is met with an impudent 'In what way?' One mark of backsliding is blindness. Another is the tendency to question everything—even the most elementary of spiritual truths and duties. Little wonder that this book is full of questions. 'In what way?' commences seven such questions:

(a) In what way have you loved us? (1:2).
(b) In what way have we despised your name? (1:6).
(c) In what way have we defiled you? (1:7).
(d) In what way have we wearied him? (2:17).
(e) In what way shall we return? (3:7)—implying, 'Have we ever left?'
(f) In what way have we robbed you? (3:8).
(g) What have we spoken against you? (3:13).

CH. 1 THE SPURNING OF HIS LOVE

CH. 2–3 THE SCORNING OF HIS LAW

CH. 4 THE SENDING OF HIS SON

The opening accusation is that God has been treated worse than any 'boss' or 'employer'. It would not suffice to treat them with an attitude of 'any old thing will do, and only when I feel like it' (see 1:6–14).

A further accusation refers to marriage. Not only were the tears of the divorced grieving the heart of God, but God's people had even resorted to marrying unbelievers yet again (2:11–16). Time and again in the Bible, God makes clear that this is forbidden (see Nehemiah's response in Nehemiah 13:27, and also 2 Corinthians 6:14).

Another accusation deals with tithing (3:8–12). Tithing was the practice of Abraham (Genesis 14:20), the promise of Jacob (Genesis 28:22), the command of Moses (Leviticus 27:30), the sin of the Jews (Malachi 3:8), and the challenge for Christians today. Giving is God's antidote to covetousness. To refrain from giving is to forfeit blessing (Malachi 3:10).

Consistent failure cried out for the coming of the Saviour. The last verse of Genesis dealt with a coffin; the last word of Malachi is 'curse'. Yet the first promise in the Old Testament (Genesis 3:15) concerned the coming of a Saviour. That is now repeated in the final promise of the Old Testament (Malachi 4). Until that promise is fulfilled God's people are exhorted to keep the commands of 'the book' (Malachi 4:4).

MARK THESE WORDS

1. Ring each 'In what way?' (or similar question).
2. Ring each 'says the LORD' (it occurs 25 times).
3. Underline 3:10. Note the condition, the reason and the promised reward. Check your own giving. Are you up to date?
4. Underline 3:16. God enjoys you 'enjoying him' with others! Do you try to do it regularly?
5. Underline the last command of the Old Testament.

The Old Testament

Conclusion

The thirty-nine books of the Old Testament were the Scriptures Jesus knew, quoted, and referred to when he said: 'O foolish ones, and slow of heart to believe in all that the prophets have spoken!' (Luke 24:25); 'The Scriptures … testify of me' (John 5:39).

Not only did God wonderfully inspire their prophetic truths, but he entrusted the sacred writings to the nation which can still trace its ancestry back to the time of Abraham. The Old Testament is safeguarded and still endorsed as the Word of God by a nation that is unbelieving regarding the Saviour, Jesus Christ.

We are about to proceed to the New Testament books, and would do well to memorize the following lines, which show how the two sections of the Bible relate to each other:

The New is in the Old concealed;
The Old is in the New revealed.

Before hurrying on, however, try to answer the following questions:
(a) Where in the OT do we read the Creation chapter?
(b) Where in the OT do we read the Passover chapter?
(c) Where in the OT do we read the main Ten Commandments chapter?
(d) Where in the OT do we read the 'shepherd' psalm?
(e) Where in the OT do we read the 'psalm of the cross'?
(f) Where in the OT do we read the 'psalm of sorrow for sin'?
(g) Where in the OT do we read the 'rejected Messiah' chapter?
(h) Which book in the OT frequently uses the word 'blood'?
(i) Which book in the OT frequently uses the word 'glory'?
(j) What is the last word in the OT?

The New Testament

Introduction

It is important to remember that 400 years of prophetic silence lay between the close of the Old Testament and the commencement of the New Testament.

Although there were no inspired writings during this period, God was not inactive.

When Jesus Christ was born in 'the fullness of the time' (Galatians 4:4) it was to a world that had witnessed the following changes:

(a) The world empires of Babylon and Persia had been succeeded first by Greece, then by Rome.

(b) The Greek empire had provided a 'world' language, which had spread a translation of the Old Testament Hebrew Scriptures throughout the Mediterranean world. This was to help with the rapid spread of Christianity in the time of the apostles.

(c) Roman rule provided law and order (Pax Romana), and excellent roads and shipping routes. These factors also were to help the rapid early spread of Christianity.

(d) The Jews of the 'Dispersion', who lived throughout the Roman empire, had built local synagogues wherever they settled in numbers.

(e) The magnificent temple at Jerusalem was built by Herod.

(f) There was tension between Jews and Samaritans—the latter claimed to be descended from Abraham, but could not prove it as the captivities had resulted in intermarriage, and the loss of family records.

(g) The Sadducees had emerged—an influential governing group of Jews, who were very liberal in matters of religion.

(h) The Pharisees had also emerged—a strict religious 'separatist' movement; they insisted on many of their own laws being kept besides those laid down by God in the Old Testament.

Into this world situation the Saviour was born.

Matthew

Know the book

Matthew was one of the twelve disciples of the Lord Jesus. He was a tax collector. He used the despised term 'tax collector' to describe himself (10:3), but nowhere else in the Bible do others call him that.

Matthew's Gospel merits being placed first of the four Gospels. It contains over sixty references to prophecy being fulfilled. It stresses the connection with the Old Testament, and underlines the truth of the couplet: 'The New is in the Old concealed; the Old is in the New revealed.'

The theme of the book is *Christ the King of the Jews*. The Old Testament said, 'Behold your King is coming to you' (Zechariah 9:9). Matthew emphasizes the authenticity, rule and reign of Christ.

Matthew opens with 'The book of "Genesis" of Jesus Christ'. The family tree is traced back to Abraham, the father of the Jewish race. The first question in the book is, 'Where is he who has been born King of the Jews?' (2:2).

The word 'kingdom' occurs frequently throughout the book (over fifty times); 'kingdom of heaven' occurs thirty-five times; 'son of David', seven times; and 'that it might be fulfilled', thirteen times. No other Gospel account uses such language so frequently.

Matthew, Mark and Luke are sometimes called the 'synoptic' Gospels. This means 'seeing the whole thing at a glance'. Matthew deals with Christ's birth (ch. 1–2); baptism (ch. 3); temptation (ch. 4); teaching (ch. 5–7); miracles (ch. 8–9) etc. It ends with controversies (ch. 21–23); two magnificent chapters on his future coming (ch. 24–25); and then his death and resurrection (ch. 26–28).

His coming in royal birth (and visit of wise men, ch. 2), his coming with authoritative teaching (especially the 'Sermon on the Mount', ch. 5–7), and his coming in future glory (ch. 24–25)—these headings can help us to remember the whole contents, as follows:

CH. 1–25 THE COMINGS OF THE KING
CH. 26–27 THE CRUCIFIXION OF THE KING
CH. 28 THE COMMISSION OF THE KING

Matthew 7 is the chapter emphasizing two choices, not three: two gates, two ways, two classes, two destinations, two trees, two fruits, two houses, two foundations, two builders and two results. We need constantly to remember that there are only two sorts of people: 'saved' and 'lost'.

Matthew 13 contains seven parables of the Kingdom.

Matthew 16 refers to 'the keys of the Kingdom' being given to Peter. Acts of the Apostles records how Peter was the first one to open the gospel door to Jews (Acts 2), Samaritans (Acts 8) and Gentiles (Acts 10). These events were the fulfilment of the promise made (Matthew 16:19).

Matthew 28 contains the Great Commission. Christ is King of all nations, and should be obeyed in all matters—and such is the emphasis in this Gospel (28:19–20).

MARK THESE WORDS

1. Ring each 'fulfilled' in the first 4 chapters.
2. Ring each 'I say to you', emphasizing the authority of the King, in chapters 5 and 6.
3. In chapter 6 ring each 'when'. The chapter encourages secret discipleship in three matters. What are they?
4. Ring each 'blessed' in chapter 5, and each 'woe' in chapter 23.
5. Ring each 'all' in 28:18–20. Can you see four instead of three?

Mark

Know the book

Mark was not one of the twelve disciples, but lived in Jerusalem, knew Peter and the other disciples (Acts 12:12–13) and helped for a while on the first missionary journey of Paul and Barnabas (Acts 13:5).

Mark wrote for Romans, and consequently in several places he defined Jewish terms.

The theme of the book is *Christ the Servant of Jehovah*. The Old Testament said, 'Behold, my Servant' (Isaiah 52:13). Mark emphasized the willingness of Christ to serve and suffer.

The key verse of the book is 10:45: 'The Son of Man did not to come to be served, but to serve, and to give his life a ransom for many.' An apt summary of the book is also found in Peter's words when he addressed Roman people in Acts 10:38.

It is interesting to note that none of the four Gospel writers ever described Christ, or gave their thoughts and opinions of him. They merely set him forth. They let him speak and act for himself. Mark lays special emphasis on Christ's activity.

The word translated 'immediately' or 'at once' occurs over forty times. 'And' occurs over 1,300 times, emphasizing the brisk pace of the brief ministry of Christ.

An early Moravian motto, placed underneath a picture of an ox standing between a plough and an altar, said 'Ready for either'. Jesus Christ, as God's Servant, was ready to serve or to be slain.

CH. 1–13 THE SERVICE OF THE SERVANT
CH. 14–16 THE SACRIFICE OF THE SERVANT

Mark demonstrates the skill of the artist by which material he has included, and which he has omitted. There is no reference to the family tree of Christ— for who is interested in the background of a slave? The book also includes the fact the Jesus was called a 'carpenter', worked seven miracles on the Sabbath, and often refers to the 'hands' of Christ—the symbol of service.

Mark does not refer to Christ as 'the Lord' until after his resurrection (1:3 is a quotation from prophecy, and in 9:24, the context makes clear that 'Lord' is on the level of 'Sir').

Mark also omits the cry from the cross, 'It is finished!' Instead, he concludes his book with an emphasis on 'the Lord [still] working' with his people as they preach the gospel (16:20).

Mark not only portrays Christ as the perfect Servant, but also as the pattern Servant. 1 Peter 2:21 says, 'Christ … (left) us an example that you should follow his steps.'

MARK THESE WORDS

1. Ring each 'immediately' in the book. 'Do it now' is always good advice.
2. Ring each 'and' or 'then' which starts a new chapter.
3. Mark 5 records 3 healings. Underline the commands Christ gave concerning each person after the healing. Do they contain lessons for the new Christian?
4. In Mark 9:43–50 ring each 'hell', and underline each part referring to unquenchable fire. Surely these verses contain one reason for any servant to be spurred on to serve!
5. Write the following words in brackets by Mark 16:15: 'Go (personally) into all the world (extensively) and preach the gospel (evangelistically)'. At the end add 'and make disciples (scripturally).' (See Matthew 28:19, margin.)

Luke

Know the book

Luke was not one of the twelve disciples. He helped Paul on his missionary journeys, and wrote both this Gospel and Acts of the Apostles. In the former he records much of the miraculous ministry of Christ; in the latter he records the miraculous ministry of the apostles, much of which he witnessed. It is interesting to note that he was a doctor, and his own medical profession is sanctioned and honoured in the Bible by his being called 'the beloved physician' (Colossians 4:14).

Luke was a Gentile, and wrote for the non-Jews. He was suited for the task. His is the Gospel for the outcast. Only Luke records the stories of 'The good Samaritan' (ch. 10), 'The tax collector at prayer' (ch. 18), 'The prodigal Son' (ch. 15), 'Zacchaeus' (ch. 19) and 'The dying thief' (ch. 23).

The theme of the book is *Christ the ideal Man*. The Old Testament said, 'Behold, the Man' (Zechariah 6:12). Luke portrays Christ as the one who came to sympathize, share, and suffer to save men and women of all sorts. The key verse is 19:10: 'The Son of Man has come to seek and to save that which was lost.'

Luke commences with two chapters devoted to the birth and early years of Christ. The family tree is traced back to Adam, the father of the human race. 'The King' was visited by foreign ambassadors in Matthew 2, but 'The Son of Man' in Luke is born in humble surroundings, and receives working men from the nearby hillside (ch. 2).

Christ's prayer life comes to prominence in this Gospel. Everyone needs to pray. Prayer is the expression of human dependency on God. 'Lord, teach us to pray' only occurs in this Gospel (11:1). Here, also, are the only accounts of 'The importunate friend' (ch. 11), 'The persistent widow' and 'The tax collector and the Pharisee' (ch. 18), all of which contain teaching on prayer.

Luke includes many references to 'widows', 'women', 'poor' and 'only' children. The sympathetic heart overlooks none.

Luke includes the only Gospel account of a 'deathbed conversion' (ch.

23). There is one such story in the Bible, that none need despair; there is only one, that none should presume.

Luke opened his book by declaring that he wanted to give an orderly account of the life of Christ (1:3). He wanted his readers to be sure of the facts (1:4). The first two chapters contain four songs of praise and glory. The world has been singing ever since.

CH. 1–19 THE SEEKING SAVIOUR
CH. 20–24 THE SUFFERING SAVIOUR

MARK THESE WORDS

1. Ring each time 'Holy Spirit' occurs in the first 4 chapters. Such references fade after Christ comes into view saying 'The Spirit of the LORD is upon me' (4:18).
2. Number the 10 prayers, or times of prayer, when found in chapters 3, 5, 6, 9 (two), 11, 22 (two), 23 and 24.
3. Ring each 'lost' and 'found' in chapter 15.
4. Ring 'only son' (7:12), 'only daughter' (8:42) and 'only child' (9:38). Do you have a loved one you are praying for with similar intensity?
5. Luke wanted his reader to know the 'certainty' of what he was writing about (1:4). Ring each 'certain' in the book (it occurs over 40 times). His last 'certainly' summarizes the book: 'Certainly this was a righteous Man!' (23:47).

John

Know the book

John was one of the twelve disciples. With his brother James, he left the fishing business of his father Zebedee to follow Christ (Matthew 4:21–22). He was known as 'the disciple whom Jesus loved' and wrote four other books of the New Testament (1, 2 and 3 John, and Revelation).

John is the last of the four Gospels. Matthew wrote for the Jew, Mark for the Roman, Luke for the Greek, but John for the whole world. The famous verse of John 3:16 is called 'the Gospel in a nutshell', and it commences: 'For God so loved the world ...'

The theme of the book is *Christ the Son of God*. The Old Testament said, 'Behold your God' (Isaiah 40:9). The key verse is 20:31, which gives the purpose of the book: 'That you may believe that Jesus is the Christ, the Son of God; and that believing you may have life in his name.'

Matthew was concerned with the coming of a promised Saviour, Mark with the life of a powerful Saviour, and Luke with the grace of a perfect Saviour; but John was concerned with the possession of a personal Saviour (see also John 1:11–12).

John contains no family tree of Christ. His opening words are: 'In the beginning was the Word' (1:1). That is all one can say about the background of God.

The first three Gospels (the 'synoptics') record when and how Christ came; John emphasizes who he was, and why he came.

CH. 1–12 THE PUBLIC WORDS OF CHRIST

CH. 13–16 THE PRIVATE WORDS OF CHRIST

CH. 19–21 THE PARDONING WORK OF CHRIST

John 2 contains the first miracle of Christ (so stories of miracles in his childhood are pure myth). This miracle typifies the power of God to change the nature within; it also contains the only command of Mary in the Bible: 'Whatever he says to you, do it' (v. 5).

John includes seven witnesses to Christ's deity: John the Baptist (1:34),

Nathanael (1:49), Peter (6:69), Martha (11:27), Thomas (20:28), John (20:31) and Christ himself (10:36).

John includes seven miracles before the resurrection, testifying to Christ's deity (chapters 2, 4, 5, 6 (two), 9 and 11).

John includes seven 'I am' claims testifying to deity (chapters 6, 8, 10 (two), 11, 14 and 15).

John alone of the Gospel authors includes the cry from the cross, 'It is finished!' God himself accomplished our redemption.

MARK THESE WORDS

1. Deity is stressed in this book. Ring each occasion where Christ refers to God as his 'Father' (occurring 35 times).
2. Definiteness is stressed in this book. Ring each occasion where Christ says, 'Most assuredly' (occurring 25 times).
3. Decision is stressed in this book. Ring each occasion where the word 'believe' is used (it occurs 98 times).
4. Think up titles and write them at the beginning of each chapter. The 'I am' claims can help with several, such as chapter 10: The good Shepherd. Others could be: (ch. 3) The divine Teacher, (ch. 4) The Soulwinner, (ch. 13) The humble Servant, (ch. 17) The great Intercessor, (ch. 18) The model Sufferer, (ch. 19) The uplifted Saviour, and (ch. 21) The Restorer of the penitent.
5. Underline each work of the Holy Spirit in chapters 14–16. The clue is often found after the words 'he will'.

Acts

Know the book

The Acts of the Apostles was written by Luke (compare 1:1 with Luke 1:3). The Bantu title for it is 'Words concerning deeds'.

Acts concentrates on the ministries of the two apostles Peter and Paul. It emphasizes the continuing acts of the risen Christ, by his Spirit, through chosen people. It also contains acts of Satan.

Acts has as its theme the extension of 'the faith' from merely a Jewish national set-up to an international world institution. The key verse is 1:8, which teaches four things clearly:
(a) The central subject of Christian witness is Christ.
(b) The exclusive source of Christian witness is the church.
(c) The widening sphere of Christian witness is the world.
(d) The unfailing secret of Christian witness is the Holy Spirit.

Acts deals first with home missions in Jerusalem, then neighbouring missions in Judea and Samaria, then finally overseas missions, reaching the capital of the empire, Rome, in the last chapter. The first twelve chapters concentrate on missions near to home: the apostle is Peter, the base is Jerusalem and the emphasis is Jewish. The last sixteen chapters deal with missions overseas: the apostle is Paul, the base is Antioch and the emphasis is Gentile.

CH. 1–7 JERUSALEM

CH. 8–12 JUDEA AND SAMARIA

CH. 13–28 THE UTTERMOST PARTS

Acts records the Holy Spirit coming on Jews (ch. 2), Samaritans (ch. 8), Gentiles (ch. 10) and proselytes (ch. 19). It also includes an account of a eunuch being converted (he could not be accepted into the Jewish faith). All accepted Christ; Christ accepted all. 'Whoever' is the gospel word for Jew (2:21) and Gentile (10:43).

Acts has three references to 'tongues' (chapters 2, 10 and 19). In all three cases the context shows that they were known foreign languages.

Acts reveals that the Holy Spirit indwells the new believer, and that baptism, laying-on of hands, and 'tarrying meetings' are not conditions of receiving him (see 10:45–48).

Acts 8–10 recounts conversions of three individuals. They came from Africa, Asia and Europe. They were in civil service, religious service and military service. They were descendants of Ham, Shem and Japheth (Genesis 6:10). Together they exemplify the 'whoever' emphasis again: no continent of origin, colour, racial background or job disqualifies a person from coming to Christ.

Acts records three missionary journeys of Paul (ch. 13–14; 16–18:22 and 18:23–21:17). There follows the journey to Rome and his period in prison there. These chapters contain the background material to Paul's letters. Among the last verses of the book is 28:28, which repeats one of the main purposes for it being written. No mention is made of the death of Paul. At the end, he is still ministering. Through the legacy of his letters, God is still using him today.

MARK THESE WORDS

1. 'Witnessing is the whole work for the whole church for the whole age' (Dr A. T. Pierson). Ring each word 'witness' in Acts.
2. Ring each word 'church' or 'churches' (27 occurrences). In Acts the 'church' is always people—never buildings.
3. Ring each reference to the 'Holy Spirit' (seventy occurrences); note the seven references to being 'filled with the Spirit'.
4. There are seventeen sermons or addresses, some long, some short. Number each one. Look out for the frequent references to Christ, prophetic fulfilment, his death and resurrection.
5. In chapter 15 a vital issue is dealt with. Write this title by it: 'Charter of the Christian faith'.

Romans

Know the book

Romans is the first of twenty-one New Testament letters, or epistles. Those written by Paul are placed first in the Bible. His letters to various churches precede his letters to individuals.

Romans is a letter written by a Hebrew in Greek from a Greek city (Corinth) to the Romans. The inscription on Christ's cross was in Hebrew, Greek and Latin (John 19:20), the languages of religion, culture and government. The letter to Romans represents them all.

Romans is 'the chief book of the New Testament' (Luther). Calvin said, 'It opened the door to all the treasures in the Scriptures.' Its theme is summarized in its early words, 'The just shall live by faith' (1:17). It was the clear understanding of what this means that caused the Reformation. The contents of Romans have brought us the gospel we rejoice in today.

Romans was not the first church letter to be written, but it is fittingly placed first. Leon Tucker wisely remarked:

Until we know the Righteousness of Romans, we cannot move on to …
the Order of Corinthians
the Liberty of Galatians
the Calling of Ephesians
the Joy of Philippians
the Head of Colossians
the Coming One of Thessalonians, or
the Substance of Hebrews.

Romans is divided into three sections: doctrinal, historical and practical. It deals with the salvation problem, the Semitic problem and the sanctification problem. It is concerned with getting right with God, thinking right about the Jews, and living right as Christians. It starts with the hell of sin, finishes with the heaven of holiness, and points the way from the one to the other.

CH. 1–8 GETTING RIGHT

CH. 9–11 THINKING RIGHT

CH. 12–16 LIVING RIGHT

Romans 1–3:20 declares that 'Everyone is guilty' (3:9,19) in spite of having the light of creation (1:20), conscience (2:15) and even the law (2:18). Romans 3:20 declares, 'The law cannot save'. The next verses declare, 'Faith in Christ does save!' Christians who *know* this truth should *reckon* on it, and *present* themselves to a holy life accordingly. (Check out the words in italics in Romans 6.)

Romans concludes with practical advice on how Christians should live as individuals, members of society, and members of God's people. Correct doctrine always leads to correct behaviour.

MARK THESE WORDS

1. Ring each 'righteousness' or 'righteous' (over sixty times).
2. Certain sins are not a cause of God giving people up, but a sign that he has already done so. Underline 'God gave them up' in chapter 1 (it occurs three times).
3. Romans 7 deals with the personal struggle with indwelling sin. Ring each 'I' in verses 7 to 25.
4. Romans 8 starts with 'no condemnation' and finishes with 'no separation'. There is hardly a reference in the book to the Holy Spirit before this chapter, but many here—ring each time the word 'Spirit' occurs. Things are different when he comes.
5. Thank God that the Jews brought us both the Bible and the Saviour. Can you find seven blessings or privileges the Jews have had, according to chapter 9?

1 Corinthians

Know the book

1 Corinthians was written by Paul to a church born during his eighteen months' ministry in Corinth, at the end of his second missionary journey (Acts 18:11). Dean Farrar said of Corinth: 'It was the Vanity Fair of the Roman Empire; at once the London and Paris of the first century.' Some of the Christian converts were still influenced by the 'wrongdoing or wicked crimes' (Acts 18:14) which surrounded them.

1 Corinthians was Paul's response to a letter to him asking questions about church order (see 7:1). In the first six chapters, however, Paul tackled disorders they had not written about (1:11).

CH. 1–6 REPROVING DISORDERLY CONDUCT

CH. 7–15 PROMOTING ORDERLY CONDUCT

1 Corinthians emphasizes sanctification, as Romans emphasizes justification. It corrects faults in living, whereas Romans corrects faults in thinking. Paul prepared his readers for his appeal to live holy and orderly lives by describing them as those 'called to be saints' (1:2).

The first four chapters of 1 Corinthians deal with party strife. Fan clubs of popular preachers, carnal splits and any conceited 'denominational' spirit are roundly condemned. In 2:14–3:4 three types of men are referred to: the 'natural' man, who is unconverted and cannot understand spiritual matters; the 'carnal' man, who is the immature Christian ruled by a natural viewpoint rather than a spiritual one; and the 'spiritual' man, who is the mature Christian whose thinking and life are governed by the Holy Spirit. It is carnal, not spiritual, Christians who cause:

(a) Divisions and splits among God's true people (ch. 1–4).

(b) Tolerance of wrong sexual standards (ch. 5).

(c) Insistence on law-court justice over disagreements (ch. 6).

1 Corinthians 7 starts with the word 'Now'. It marks the beginning of Paul's teaching on the questions the Corinthians had asked. He begins each

new subject with the same or similar word, helping to mark the different sections:

(a) Marriage ('Now'—7:1).

(b) Meats ('Now'—8:1).

(c) Meetings ('Now'—(1) 11:2 Women's ministry, and (2) 11:17 Lord's Table).

(d) Manifold gifts ('Now'—12:1).

(e) Mystery of resurrection ('Moreover' and 'Now'—15:1,12).

(f) Money ('Now'—16:1).

Paul answers each question from a spiritual viewpoint, not from a sociological or psychological one. For example, wrong sex is not wrong because it damages society or the individual, but rather because it defiles the temple of God (the human body—6:15–20); similarly, 'meats' (representative of so many questionable matters) should be avoided because of a bad example to weaker Christians.

The famous 'love' chapter (ch. 13) is central in the three chapters dealing with the contention about gifts. It is possible to have gifts and a poor spiritual condition, but it is not possible to have 'love' and a poor spiritual condition.

MARK THESE WORDS

1. Ring each 'do you not know' (it occurs ten times).
2. Underline Paul's motto in 9:22 and ring each 'that I might win' in verses 19–22.
3. The Old Testament has been written so that Christians can learn from its examples. Underline 10:11, and ring 'nor' in 10:7–10.
4. In 15:12–19, ring each 'if' (seven times). Seven tragic results follow if there is no resurrection from the dead. Find them in these verses, and number them appropriately.

2 Corinthians

Know the book

2 Corinthians is connected with some of the material in the previous letter Paul wrote to the Corinthians. Most of his letters were follow-up letters to his preaching; this was a follow-up letter to his previous writing.

'Comfort' is a key word in 2 Corinthians. It occurs at the beginning of the letter (1:3) and at the end (13:11). Paul had been tough in criticizing sins for which there had been no signs of repentance. In this second letter, he is tender in consoling sinners who had subsequently shown signs of repentance. There is a time to discipline an offending Christian. There is also a time to restore to fellowship.

2 Corinthians deals with additional problems as well. Paul had been opposed while at Corinth (Acts 18:12–13). The chief Jew had been converted, but others had been antagonistic. This letter shows that Paul's personal integrity had been questioned, and his apostolic authority undermined.

The former letter to the Corinthians had shown Paul as a pattern preacher: he emphasized the Christ of the cross, amid people clamouring for miraculous signs or intellectual debate (1 Corinthians 1:21–24). This latter letter shows Paul as a pattern apostle: enduring a daily dying (4:10–12), evangelizing with the appeal of an ambassador (5:20) among teachers more interested in their own authoritarianism, wealth and position (11:20).

Ch. 1–7 Testifying to sufficiency
Ch. 8–9 Encouraging generosity
Ch. 10–13 Defending authority

The motives behind and the manner of Christian giving are dealt with in two challenging chapters (8 and 9). Giving proves the sincerity of love (8:8), follows the example of Christ (8:9), helps towards equality (8:14), and answers accusing onlookers (8:21). Giving should be according to a personal plan (9:7), not resented or forced (9:7), cheerfully done (9:7), generously done (9:6,13), and directed to those causes where there is need (9:12) and which glorify God (9:12–13).

Human leaders are often known for their affluence, intelligence, and the respect in which they are held. Paul claimed poverty, hardship and abuse, and the need for revelation as the marks of his apostolic authority. He had a remarkable 'experience' (ch. 12), but mentioned nothing about it until compelled to—and that was after fourteen years of keeping it quiet. God used a 'thorn' and unanswered prayer to keep him humble and thereby useful (12:7–9).

MARK THESE WORDS

1. Ring each 'comfort' or 'comforted' in the book.
2. Ring each 'consolation' and 'sorrow' in chapters 1, 2 and 7.
3. The best people to comfort those with problems are those who have had the same problems themselves, and have derived comfort from God. That is why Job's comforters failed to comfort him, whereas Job has comforted millions. Underline 1:4, which teaches this fact. Those who want to bless others often have to graduate in the school of suffering.
4. Ring the words 'another' and 'different' in 11:4. What three alternatives is the Christian to beware of?
5. Underline 13:14, and note that it is a popular 'benediction' today.
6. Do you send 'follow-up' letters? Are you up to date in your correspondence? Should a second letter be sent to anybody? Do it now. Determine to send a 'comfort' card when next you hear of someone seriously ill or recently bereaved.

Galatians

Know the book

Galatians was written to a group of churches in an area known today as Turkey. Paul visited the area during each of his three missionary journeys.

Galatians was written because there had been a serious defection of his converts to 'cult' teaching which followed on the heels of Paul's pioneering efforts. The trouble came from Jews teaching that the initiation rite of becoming a Jew (circumcision) and a strict observance of their laws were essential for salvation. The book is very relevant today. There are 'initiation ceremonies' and 'traditional observances' besides Jewish ones. Certain denominations and cult groups do not teach that we are saved by 'Christ alone', but by 'Christ and …' Some emphasize 'Christ and christening', 'Christ and baptism', 'Christ and confirmation', 'Christ and the Mass and penance', or 'Christ and seventh-day observance'. This book exposes the error of them all.

Dr Graham Scroggie called Galatians 'the Magna Carta of Christian emancipation'. It was Luther's favourite book. It deals with justification by faith without the deeds of the law. God raised up Moses to deliver the children of Israel from Egyptian bondage, and Paul to deliver the Christian church from Jewish bondage. This major dispute was settled once and for all by the Church council meeting recorded in Acts 15.

Galatians uses the teaching of 'justification' to combat error, while Romans deals with it systematically. Romans emphasizes the Christian's standing; Galatians insists that Christians stand (5:1). Romans was written to ground Christians in doctrine, Corinthians to guide them in practice, and Galatians to guard them from error.

Galatians is divided into three sections: personal, doctrinal and practical. The first deals with revelation, the second with justification, and the third with sanctification.

'Gospel' means 'good news'. God's news is so good, man would never have guessed or worked it out. It had to be revealed (1:12).

The key verse is 2:16. It is supported by 2:21: If there was a way of salvation besides Christ, Christ's death would have been unnecessary and he would not have died.

The book is full of words that are contrasted: 'gospel' with 'another gospel', 'works' with 'faith', 'law' with 'promise', 'servant' with 'son', 'slave' with 'free', and 'flesh' with 'Spirit'.

Galatians 5:4 says that these Christians had 'fallen from grace'. The context shows that Paul was not arguing that they had lost their security of salvation so much as their sanity of mind (3:1).

MARK THESE WORDS

1. Ring each 'works', 'law', 'faith' and 'promise' (over 60 times).
2. Galatians 3:1–5 asks six questions; 3:6–14 contains six Bible quotes. Underline these quotations. Remember that it's good to answer with Scripture.
3. Galatians 5:17–23 was summarized by Guy King as 'From the slum to the orchard'. Underline the seventeen sins of unclean living, and the nine-fold fruit of the Spirit.
4. Paul had given up 'Judaism' (1:13–14) but was not opposed to the 'true Jew' who had been completed by being converted to Christ (6:16). In chapter 6, note verses which show that Paul is not opposed to 'law', 'work', 'burden', etc., either. The Christian is called to liberty, but not to licence.

Ephesians

Know the book

Ephesians was written to the church at Ephesus and possibly the surrounding area. Paul visited there briefly on his second missionary journey, but spent over two years there on his third one (Acts 18:19–20; 19:10).

Ephesians was not written because of doctrinal error or moral laxity. It was a glorious church; nevertheless in later years it left its first love (Revelation 2:4). We do not have to wait for special needs to arise before writing someone a letter of encouragement.

Ephesians is the complementary New Testament book to the book of Joshua in the Old Testament. Joshua's theme is the national blessings God bestowed on the Hebrews in the earthly place of Canaan; Ephesians' theme is the spiritual blessings God has bestowed on Christians in heavenly places 'in Christ'.

Ephesians is one of Paul's prison letters. Towards the end of his life, while imprisoned at Rome, he wrote this letter, Philippians, Colossians and Philemon. Ezekiel in Babylon, John on Patmos and Bunyan in Bedford also proved the benefits of similar times when they were themselves confined. God sometimes silences his servants for a period so that the world can hear more clearly what they say.

Ephesians also contains two of Paul's tremendous prison prayers. The emphasis of the first is 'that you may know' (1:18), while that of the second is more that they might 'have' (3:14–21). David, Solomon and Daniel were among those who knelt in prayer. The hard prison floor did not stop Paul from doing the same (3:14).

Ephesians has as its theme the magnificent blessings of the church—Christ's redeemed people. The church is viewed as Christ's body (1:22–23 and 4:15), building (2:21–22) and bride (5:25). Each Christian is linked to Christ in a living, lasting and loving union.

Ephesians speaks of the fullness of God (3:19), Christ (4:13) and the Spirit (5:18). Each Christian united to and filled by such a God will experience transformation by him as well. High calling never goes hand in hand with low living. In Ephesians, therefore, doctrine moves to practice; belief leads to behaviour; creed influences conduct.

CH. 1–3 THE CHRISTIAN'S HEAVENLY WEALTH

CH. 4–6 THE CHRISTIAN'S EARTHLY WALK

Ephesians deals with the walk of the world (2:2) and the wicked (4:17), and teaches that the walk of the Christian should be beneficial (2:10), worthy (4:1), loving (5:2), clean (5:8), and wise (5:15).

Ephesians 2 is the Christian's biography. Is it your testimony? Ephesians 3:5 defines the biblical use of the word 'mystery'. It means something not known until God revealed it. The book refers to the mysteries of God's will (1:9), Christ (3:4), the church (5:32), and the gospel (6:19).

MARK THESE WORDS

1. Ring each 'in' in chapter 1 (it occurs over 90 times in the book).
2. God does not bless us according to what we deserve. Ring each 'according to' in chapter 1 to find out some of his reasons.
3. Ring each 'walk' (it occurs 8 times).
4. The book is full of 'Christ'. Ring each occurrence. It is even more full of him if you count 'him' and 'he', etc.
5. Underline 5:18. The remainder of the book shows some of the effects for Christians of being 'filled with the Spirit'—in their hearts, homes, domestic and social lives, and in their prayerful and evangelistic burdens (see 5:18–6:20).

Philippians

Know the book

Philippians was written to the first church that was founded in Europe. Paul visited there briefly on his second missionary journey (Acts 16).

Philippians is one of Paul's prison letters, written from his Roman jail. He had also been in jail while at Philippi. He had had the joy of leading his jailer to Christ. While imprisoned in Rome he also led people to Christ (Philemon 10; see also 4:22).

Philippians was written as a 'thank you' letter for financial support (4:10–20) and also because of the trouble in the church. The problem was neither doctrinal nor moral, but one of a personality clash between two women (4:2).

Paul did not side with either party. He loved 'all' (1:8), prayed for 'all' (1:4) and wrote to 'all' (1:1) Before dealing directly with the problem, he referred to 'one mind' and 'one spirit' (1:27) and 'one accord' (2:1–3). His comments on murmurings and disputings (2:14) and maturity (3:15–16) also laid the foundation for his appeal for unity, not to mention the magnificent reference to Christ's example (2:1–11).

Philippians is a book for complainers. The key verse is 4:4: 'Rejoice in the Lord always. Again I will say, rejoice!' The key words are 'joy' and 'rejoice'. They occur in each chapter. Joy is different from happiness. The latter is like calm on the surface of the sea—it depends on the circumstances; the former is like the calm to be found deep down—unruffled in spite of circumstances. Paul could rejoice, although he experienced suffering and sorrow (2:27).

Philippians 1 shows that Paul had joy in prayer (1:4), joy in knowing Christ was preached (1:18), and joy even in his sufferings, because he realized they were promoting evangelism (1:12–18).

Ch. 1 Christ our life
Ch. 2 Christ our example
Ch. 3 Christ our goal
Ch. 4 Christ our strength

Philippians 2 records the example of Christ (vv. 5–11), then of Paul being willing to die in service (v. 17), of Timothy, who lived for others (vv. 20–22), and of Epaphroditus, who was sick and almost died through serving Christ (vv. 25–30). These all followed Christ, who became 'obedient to the point of death' for the sake of others (v. 8). Paul had joy when he knew that other Christians followed like that (v. 2).

Philippians 3 shows that Paul rejoiced in Christ. All his goals in life were related to knowing him and living for him (vv. 8–14). He wanted other Christians to have the same goals as himself (v. 17).

Philippians 4 contains the appeal for unity (v. 2) and the thanks for support (vv. 10–20), and concludes with a benediction involving the word 'grace' which is a mark of all Paul's conclusions (v. 23).

MARK THESE WORDS
1. Ring each 'joy' and 'rejoice' (they occur 16 times).
2. Ring each 'all', especially in chapter 1.
3. Number the seven steps Christ took in order to save us in 2:6–8.
4. Number the seven ambitions of Paul in 3:8–14. Ring the 3 occurrences of 'that I may'.
5. We must work out what God has worked in. Compare 1:6 with 2:12–13. Also check what God is going to do, in 3:21.
6. Underline 1:21; 4:13 and 4:19. Sufficient strength and supply is guaranteed for the supreme purpose of living for Christ.

Colossians

Know the book

Colossians was one of Paul's prison letters written from Rome.

Colossians shows the greatness of Paul's heart, and his concern even for churches he had not visited (2:1). Colosse was a small place, about 1,000 miles from Rome.

Colossians was written at the same time as Ephesians. In many ways they are twin letters. They contain similar expressions. Yet the variations are also interesting (note the 'Spirit-filled man' of Ephesians 5:18 is the 'Scripture-filled man' of Colossians 3:16). Ephesians emphasizes the church of Christ; Colossians emphasizes the Christ of the church.

Colossians deals with Christianity being corrupted by the double error of tradition and philosophy (this latter means 'love of wisdom')—see 2:8. Tradition always leads to legalism and formalism (2:8–17); philosophy can lead to mysticism and asceticism (2:18–23).

Colossians is relevant today. Eastern mysticism, transcendental meditation and interest in the 'spirit' world are joining the old errors of saint worship and spiritism. Modern communes can be as ascetic as medieval monastic orders. Wrong views of Christianity are usually born out of wrong views of Christ. The opening chapter focuses magnificent attention on him as the pre-existent One, the pre-eminent One, the Creator, and the only and all-sufficient Saviour who has already reconciled believers to God through his death on the cross (1:21–22) and indwells all believers (1:27), who are thereby 'complete in him' (2:10).

Paul warned the Colossians to be on their guard against deceitful teachers whose arguments sounded good (2:4), but which had no foundation apart from empty speculation (2:18). It is significant that he addresses the church as 'faithful brethren' (1:2), and commends Epaphras, Tychicus and Onesimus as 'faithful' also (1:7; 4:7,9).

Colossians contains the following comments on 'wisdom' by Paul:
(a) True wisdom is his prayer for them (1:9).
(b) True wisdom in teaching comes from revelation (1:28,26).
(c) True wisdom is ultimately to be found only in Christ (2:3).

(d) True wisdom is different from 'an appearance of wisdom' (2:23).
(e) True wisdom is channelled through Scripture (3:16).
(f) True wisdom should govern the Christian's behaviour (4:5).

Colossians 3 is the Christian's 'changing room'. Having 'put off' one life in principle, we should put it off in practice; having 'put on' a new life in principle, we should put it on in practice. Being 'dead', we should 'put to death'; being 'risen', we should 'seek those things which are above' (see vv. 1–15). Christians are no better than worldly philosophers if their lives do not match up to their claims.

MARK THESE WORDS

1. The book is full of Christ. Ring each 'Christ', and each 'he', 'him' and 'his' which refers to Christ.
2. Ring each 'wisdom' in the book, and 'philosophy' in 2:8.
3. Ring each 'put off' and 'put on' in 3:1–15 and in Ephesians 4:21–32.
4. Underline 3:16a. Are you a 'Scripture-filled' person? How are your memory verses coming on?
5. Underline 4:12. The Greek word describing Epaphras' praying is 'agonizomai'. Do we ever agonize in prayer for others? How are you getting on with your prayer diary? Update it now.

1 Thessalonians

Know the book

The Thessalonian letters were written by Paul. They were probably the earliest New Testament letters to be written.

The Thessalonian letters were part of Paul's follow-up ministry to a church he had founded in Thessalonica in approximately AD 50 on his second missionary journey (Acts 17:1–10). Paul had been a Christian about fifteen years by this time, and had stayed in Thessalonica only a month or so, yet he shows in these letters the richness of doctrinal content contained in his early evangelism.

The Thessalonian letters contain frequent references to 'God' (over fifty times) and 'Christ' or a similar title (over fifty times.) They have clear teaching on the death of Christ, his resurrection, the gospel, salvation by faith, sanctification, the works of the Spirit and of Satan, and extensive details of the return of Christ.

The first four church letters in the Bible (Romans, 1 & 2 Corinthians and Galatians) have a great deal of teaching on Christ and the cross. The next three (Ephesians, Philippians and Colossians) have an emphasis on Christ and the church. The last two, the Thessalonian letters, stress Christ and his coming again.

The Second Coming of Christ is mentioned 318 times in the 260 chapters of the New Testament. On average, one verse in every twenty deals with this subject.

1 Thessalonians refers to the Second Coming in each chapter:

In ch. 1 the Second Coming is an *inspiring* hope.

In ch. 2 the Second Coming is an *encouraging* hope.

In ch. 3 the Second Coming is a *purifying* hope.

In ch. 4 the Second Coming is a *comforting* hope.

In ch. 5 the Second Coming is a *rousing* hope.

1 Thessalonians also deals with Paul's results in evangelism (ch. 1), his principles in evangelism (ch. 2) and his follow-up concern (ch. 3–5).

In 1 Thessalonians 1, verse 3 is explained by verses 9–10:

(a) 'work of faith' = 'turned to God from idols';

(b) 'labour of love' = 'to serve the living and true God';

(c) 'patience of hope' = 'to wait for his Son from heaven'.

It is a pity the Ephesians lost this faith, love and hope (Revelation 2:2).

1 Thessalonians 2 stresses that the evangelist's message must be true, his motives pure, and his methods above board.

1 Thessalonians 4 deals with a worry they had about believers who had died. Heathen graves had written on them: 'After death, no reviving; after grave, no meeting.' Paul comforted the Thessalonians by correcting the error that was influencing them (4:13–18). The return of Christ, the resurrection of the body, the rapture of the saints, and the reunion of all the saved, are doctrines used to correct error and comfort the bereaved Christian.

MARK THESE WORDS

1. Ring the word 'God' each time it occurs.

2. Paul shunned any authoritarian attitude, although he preached with authority. Notice his strong appeal to 'brethren'. Ring each time the word comes. (Including 'brother' and 'brotherly', the total is over 20.)

3. Ring the number of each verse which deals with the Second Coming in one aspect or another. Each chapter has at least one verse dealing with the subject.

2 Thessalonians

Know the book

2 Thessalonians extends the teaching of 1 Thessalonians, with particular reference to the Second Coming.

2 Thessalonians introduces a note of caution about the time of this event. In 1 Thessalonians Paul taught, 'He is coming!' In 2 Thessalonians he teaches, 'He has not come yet!' In the earlier letter, Paul taught that the coming would be 'as a thief' (1 Thessalonians 5:2), but by that he did not mean 'secretly', but 'suddenly' or 'unexpectedly'. In 2 Thessalonians, he makes clear that by 'suddenly' he did not mean 'immediately', but 'quickly'. In a similar way, 'unexpected' does not mean 'unanticipated', but 'uncertain as to precise time'.

2 Thessalonians is relevant today, with some cults maintaining that Christ has already come secretly, while others insist that precise date-fixing is possible.

CH. 1 THE COMING OF THE LOVELY ONE

CH. 2 THE COMING OF THE LAWLESS ONE

CH. 3 THE COMING OF THE LAZY ONE

2 Thessalonians 1 refers to the Second Coming as a comfort for the persecuted, and a terror for the unconverted. Christ will return visibly from heaven (v. 7) with angels (v. 7), bringing judgement on the unconverted (v. 8), who will be for ever banished from his presence (v. 9). Christians are already 'accepted in the Beloved' (Ephesians 1:6), but on that day they will admire and adore the Beloved (v. 10) and henceforth will be for ever in the presence of the Lord (1 Thessalonians 4:17).

2 Thessalonians 2 lists seven certainties which will happen before Christ actually returns, namely:

(a) There will be a 'falling away' or apostasy (v. 3).

(b) The 'man of sin' will come (v. 3).

(c) The 'temple of God' will be desecrated (v. 4).

(d) The 'restrainer' will be withdrawn (vv. 6–7).

(e) The 'mystery of lawlessness' will increase (v. 7).

(f) The 'lawless one' will be revealed (v. 8).

(g) There will be 'signs and lying wonders' (v. 9).

These seven events are certain to happen. Their meaning is not always clear, however, and Christians have differed in trying to interpret them. A measure of obscurity, though, does encourage Christians ever to be aware of what is happening, and ever to be ready for their returning Lord.

2 Thessalonians 3 contains instructions for any Christian who refuses to work. The model church described in 1 Thessalonians 1 showed that these believers were working while waiting for the coming of the Lord. The Bible gives no grounds for giving up employment on the basis that the Lord's coming may be near. Idle busybodies are to be admonished (vv. 11,15), avoided, and should be ashamed (v. 14). They are not to be encouraged by being given support. One thing idlers should never suffer from is indigestion!

MARK THESE WORDS

1. Ring each 'God' and 'brother', as in 1 Thessalonians.
2. Note the two means to accomplish salvation (2:13). Ring the word 'sanctification' in this verse and also in 1 Thessalonians 4:3–4. The word 'holiness' in 1 Thessalonians 3:13 and 4:7 is the same in Greek. Note from the context how 'sanctification' is closely linked with clean sexual living.
3. Ring each 'command' in chapter 3 (it occurs 4 times).
4. Ring the number of each verse referring to Christ's Second Coming.

1 Timothy

Know the book

1 Timothy, 2 Timothy and Titus are the three pastoral letters. They were some of the last letters written by an ageing Paul, who was anticipating the end of his earthly ministry. They were written to leaders about church government and order. Their theme is *Christ and the congregation*. Together they form the 'minister's manual' contained within the Bible. There is a time to speak just to leaders—nobody is ever too old to learn.

Timothy is addressed by Paul as 'a true son in the faith' (1:2). He was one of Paul's converts—possibly converted during the first missionary tour (Acts 14). He joined the missionary team of the second tour (Acts 16:1–3). In the years that followed he was close to Paul and entrusted with several personal missions, one of which is referred to in 1:3.

1 Timothy 3:15 indicates the main theme of the book: 'How you ought to conduct yourself in the house of God.' The first half deals with church doctrine, prayer, the place of men and women in public worship, and those who qualify for church office. The second half is more personal and deals with the example, conduct and duties of the leader.

CH. 1–3 ORDERLY CONDUCT IN CHURCHES

CH. 4–6 EXEMPLARY CONDUCT IN LEADERS

1 and 2 Timothy emphasize the importance of 'doctrine' and 'the truth'. These are God's means of delivering from error and evil (4:16). In 'latter times' there will be a forsaking of a Bible-believing position (4:1). Leaders are to oppose this (1:3).

1 Timothy 1 is a miniature biography of Paul, converted and made both a trustee of the gospel (1:11) and an example of Christ's longsuffering and patience with undeserving sinners (1:16).

1 Timothy 3 deals with 'elders' (bishops) responsible for spiritual matters, and 'deacons' responsible for temporal matters. Paul refers to two offices only. There is no reference to some being in an office of 'priest'. In

Acts 6, being 'full of the Holy Spirit' was a condition for office; in 1 Timothy 3 this is worked out in a detailed character study.

1 Timothy 5 teaches that leaders must not show favouritism (v. 21). Advice is given regarding financial help to the needy. There is a principle of priority which should take precedence over any principle of equality (v. 16). In all giving, Christians should always investigate before they invest.

1 Timothy 6 points out errors concerning money. There were prosperity teachers maintaining that 'godliness is a means of gain' (v. 5). Timothy is told to withdraw from them. Wanting to be rich can bring sorrow and spiritual shipwreck for the Christian (v. 10). Timothy is told to flee such desires and temptations (v. 11). He is reminded that the leader is to work until Jesus comes (v. 14). Christian service is not to end with retirement.

MARK THESE WORDS

1. Ring 'doctrine', 'the faith' and 'the truth' wherever they occur in the book.
2. Underline the 'faithful sayings' in 1:15; 3:1 and 4:9. Thomas Bilney, who led the martyr Hugh Latimer to Christ, was converted through 1:15.
3. Ring each 'all' in 2:1–6 (it occurs 6 times). Do you pray for 'all' your family? 'All' your friends? 'All' you know? If not, at least try to pray for more!
4. 'Some' will depart from the faith in latter times (4:1). Ring this 'some', and wherever else it occurs.
5. Ring each 'godliness' (it occurs nine times—eight 'good' times, and once in a 'bad' context).

2 Timothy

Know the book

2 Timothy is the last letter Paul wrote which is in the Bible. Last words can be lasting words. Some of the last words of the Cornish evangelist Billy Bray were, 'Glory, glory, I'm going to heaven. Incidentally, doctor, will I see you there?' He wanted his last words to count.

2 Timothy shows that Paul was more concerned for Timothy and the future of the gospel than he was for himself. He pointed to 'the word', 'the truth' and 'the Scriptures' as authoritative. There is no reference to any apostolic successor for Paul or any other apostle.

2 Timothy 1 contains 'ashamed' three times. In Romans 1:16 Paul had declared he was not ashamed of the gospel of Christ. In this letter he says he is not ashamed of suffering for it (v. 12), that Onesiphorus is not ashamed of his being imprisoned for it (v. 16), and that Timothy should not be ashamed of either what Christ suffered, or what his servants suffer (v. 8).

2 Timothy 2 includes another realm in which the Christian leader should not be ashamed. He should be a Bible student who has a balanced grasp of 'the word of truth' (v. 15). That is one of the important conditions of being 'useful for the Master' (v. 21).

God's 'word of truth' should be held fast (1:13), studied carefully (2:15) and preached at all times (4:2).

2 Timothy 3 describes conditions in 'the last days', whereas the first letter to Timothy dealt with 'latter times'. Comparing the two passages (1 Timothy 4 and 2 Timothy 3) seems to suggest that initially 'some' will apostatize from the true faith, and that this will lead to further deterioration until 'all' are involved in self-centredness (3:2), with no true godliness (3:5), and with widespread practices of anarchy and gospel opposition (3:1–8).

2 Timothy 4 contains Paul's farewell speech. Death is referred to as a 'departure'. Like a ship being loosed from its moorings, Paul is about to go away; like somebody striking camp for the last time, he is about to go home. He had joyful anticipation at the prospect of seeing Christ (v. 8), no sense of shame because of his faithful track record (v. 7), and he urged

Timothy to follow similarly (vv. 1–5) and to be aware of the current situation relating to many individuals. The apostle was about to depart, so his final benediction included the reminder that Christ would ever remain, as would grace sufficient for every need (v. 22).

CH. 1–2 UNASHAMED STAND

CH. 3–4 UNSYMPATHETIC TIMES

MARK THESE WORDS

1. Underline Romans 1:16 and ring the 4 times 'ashamed' occurs in the first two chapters of 2 Timothy.
2. Paul was interested in individuals. Ring each different name that occurs in the letter. Count them. Do you know that many people individually in your church? Do you pray for them?
3. Three verses in this letter form another 'faithful saying'. Underline this one as well.
4. There are 5 'loves' in these two letters. The good one is in 2 Timothy 4:8: 'love' for Christ's appearing. That love will weaken the other 4 'bad' loves in 1 Timothy 6:10, 2 Timothy 3:2, 4 and 4:10.
5. Underline 3:15–17. The Bible is for every child of man (v. 15), every child of God (1 Peter 2:2) and every man of God (v.17).
6. Note that some things require us to 'fight' (1 Timothy 6:12), while others require 'flight' (2 Timothy 2:22), as Joseph did in Genesis 39:18.

Titus

Know the book

Titus is the third of the three pastoral letters Paul wrote to church leaders.

Titus had long had connections with Paul (Galatians 2:1–3). He is addressed as 'a true son in our common faith' (1:4) and was another convert from Paul's missionary work.

Titus came from a Gentile/pagan background; Timothy came from a Jewish/Christian one. Character studies show that Titus was the stronger of the two. Paul entrusted him with a leadership role in a very difficult area (1:5–16).

Titus, like the other pastoral letters, emphasizes conduct in the church, qualities to be looked for in potential leaders, and guidelines for both family and social life.

Chapter 1 indicates that Titus had been designated to 'set in order' church matters. The credentials of leadership were dependent on apostolic writing, not apostolic hands (vv. 6–9). Weymouth translates 'not self-willed' (v. 7) as 'not overfond of having his own way'.

Titus is pointed to the need for 'healthy', or 'sound', spirituality. The word is used twice in chapter 1. In chapter 2, 'sound doctrine' (v. 1), 'sound in faith' (v. 2) and 'sound speech' (v. 8) are three ingredients that go towards being a 'sound' Christian.

Titus 2 also contains some pertinent passages particularly relevant to older men and women, younger men and women, and working people. Conditions in the factory, in the home and family, and in society in general would all be better if these instructions were adhered to. It is the responsibility of Christian leadership to give clear instructions relating to Christian duties in these realms.

Paul stated when a woman should *not* teach in 1 Timothy 2:12. He now states when a woman *should* teach, in Titus 2:4. Homemaking (1 Timothy 2:4–5) and homeguiding (1 Timothy 5:14) are two frequently neglected ministries.

'Faithful sayings' occur in the pastoral letters. Titus 3:8 is yet another example. However, the word 'for' in 2:11 and 3:3 is followed in both cases by magnificent passages full of precise doctrinal content. It may be that these also form two sayings which were well known among the early Christians.

CH. 1 AN ORDERLY CHURCH

CH. 2 A SOUND CHURCH

CH. 3 A PRACTICAL CHURCH

MARK THESE WORDS

1. Ring the occasions where 'good works' occurs. 'Works' by itself adds another two occasions. Spurgeon was once asked if he was opposed to good works. He replied, 'No, nor to chimney pots—but I don't put them at the foundation!'
2. Ring the occasions where 'sound' occurs. (It means 'healthy' in this biblical context.)
3. List the eight qualities of a good Christian wife listed in chapter 2.
4. Note carefully the description of the One who is to appear gloriously (2:13). The full deity and saviourhood of Christ are clearly taught in this passage.
5. In 3:1–3 there are seven injunctions for Christians to observe and seven sinful characteristics to avoid. Place a small number by each or list them on paper.
6. Note in 2:11–14 the three tenses: past, present and future. This is an excellent passage to meditate on or to commit to memory. For speakers, it could provide an excellent basis for a gospel talk.

Philemon

Know the book

Philemon is one of Paul's four prison letters. Although it is the shortest and most personal letter, it is a spiritual masterpiece. Like a priceless miniature in the best art gallery, it must not be glossed over because of its size.

Philemon (meaning 'affectionate') was probably a convert of Paul's (v. 19) who opened his house for Christian hospitality (vv. 7,22) and meetings (v. 2).

Philemon had a slave named Onesimus (meaning 'useful'). This slave had robbed his master (vv. 11,18) and run away to Rome, where he had come into contact with Paul and been converted through his ministry (v. 10).

Philemon is a book which reveals that Paul never withdrew from soul-winning evangelism, even when old and confined to jail (v. 9). In counselling this new convert, Paul faced him with the need to apologize and make restitution. Debt dodging and duty dodging do not belong to the Christian faith. The evangelist, however, showed a magnificent example of standing alongside the new convert who had got right with God, as he faced the struggle of getting right with man. Paul had been helped himself in his early difficult days as a Christian when Barnabas had stood with him (Acts 9:27). Now the aged Paul stands alongside the converted runaway.

It was hard for Paul to send Onesimus back (v. 13), harder still for Onesimus to go back (law would have insisted on his death); but probably it was hardest for Philemon to accept Onesimus back, as Paul urged him to do.

vv. 1–7 PAUL'S PARTNERSHIP IN PRAYER

vv. 8–16 PAUL'S PLEA FOR A PRODIGAL

vv. 17–25 PAUL'S PROMISE OF PAYMENT

Philemon contains a wonderful gospel analogy, illustrating the principle of redemption. Man is God's property who has run away and offended him, robbing him of his property and honour. When saved by Christ, he is returned to God, not as a slave but as a member of the family (v. 16).

'Reckon to him my merit; reckon to me his demerit' is a summary of verses 17–18. 'Receive' occurs three times:

'Receive him' (v. 12).

'Receive him for ever' (v. 15).

'Receive him as you would me' (v. 17).

Philemon is also an illustration of the fact that the guiding principle behind Christian action should be persuasion rather than compulsion (vv. 8–9). Many phrases and words in this short letter are calculated to move the heart.

Philemon also illustrates that 'Christianizing' the master is one way of emancipating the slave. Legislation gets a man to *realize* what he should do; evangelism gets a man to *do* what he realizes he should do. Getting laws right is good; getting hearts right is better. Getting laws right achieves something; getting hearts right achieves far more. It was Paul's spiritual work of evangelizing with the gospel of Christ which ultimately transformed the social and moral outlook of the world.

MARK THESE WORDS

1. Ring each 'receive him' in the book.
2. Paul appeals to the response of love not law. Ring each 'love' or similar word.
3. Interest in individuals continues. Ring each personal name in this short letter.
4. Note that Demas was a worker at the time of writing (v. 24); he is still around in Colossians 4:14, but there is no reference to him working. By 2 Timothy 4:10 he has left the team. Note the reason why. Pray lest slowly slackening dedication leads to personal backsliding.

Hebrews

Know the book

Hebrews was most likely written by Paul. If those who question it ever show otherwise, a classic book of Scripture has not been lost—we have merely gained an additional author who was also 'moved by the Holy Spirit' (2 Peter 1:21).

Hebrews heads up the Bible section sometimes known as the 'Hebrew–Christian Letters', just as Romans commences Paul's letters. Romans emphasizes the necessity of the Christian faith; Hebrews emphasizes the superiority of the Christian faith. Romans deals with the finished work of Christ; Hebrews deals with both the finished and the unfinished works of Christ: his finished work of redemption on earth, and his continuing ministry of intercession in heaven (7:25). The Old Testament religion was based on the pattern of the Christ who was to come; Hebrews declares the religion of the Christ on whom the pattern was based. A photo of a person can be helpful, but it is unnecessary when the person is present himself—so it is with Christ. Old Testament 'shadow' has been replaced by New Testament 'substance', and 'type' has been replaced by 'antitype'. The Jewish faith has been superseded by the Christian faith. This is the emphasis of 'Hebrews' for the Hebrews.

Hebrews sets out the superiority of Christ and the Christian faith, and the peril faced by those who had emerged from Judaism who were tempted to go back to former beliefs and ritualism. The book is relevant today, not only in its Jewish application, but also wherever a person has been converted to Christ from a religion which parallels Judaism. Irrespective of the vast numbers associated with it, its extensiveness geographically, the worldwide acceptance of an organized priesthood, uniform initiation rites into membership and regular, ongoing ceremonies to keep its membership right with God—such a religion is not to be compared with the truth as it is in Christ. In this book, those who come to faith in Christ are given a fivefold warning against returning to any previous inferior beliefs and practices they were connected with.

CH. 1–2 SUPERIOR REVELATION OF CHRIST
CH. 3–10 SUPERIOR REDEMPTION OF CHRIST
CH. 11–13 SUPERIOR RESULTS OF FAITH

Hebrews systematically shows that Christ is superior to the prophets (1:1–3), angels (1:4–2:18), Moses (ch. 3), Joshua (ch. 4—called 'Jesus' in v. 8), and Aaron (ch. 5–7). The Christian faith is based on 'better promises' (ch. 8), 'better sacrifices' (ch. 9), and has a 'better' future (ch. 10).

Hebrews 11 could be called 'Faith's picture gallery'—it points to the better principle of faith.

MARK THESE WORDS

1. The whole book is based on scriptural argument, and is constantly supported by quotations. Underline each OT quote in chapters 1–3.
2. Ring each 'better' (it occurs 13 times).
3. Note the finality of Christ's completed work. In 9:7–10:14 ring each 'once' or 'one' (9 times altogether).
4. Note the 5 warning passages, and ring key words in each: 'neglect' (2:3), 'unbelief' and 'departing from' (3:12), 'fall away' (6:6), 'counted … common', 'insulted the Spirit' (10:29) and 'turn away' (12:25).
5. Note 3 *abilities* of Christ: to succour (2:18), to sympathize (4:15), and to save to the uttermost (7:25).
6. Note 3 *appearings* of Christ in 9:24–28.
7. Note 3 *absolute essentials* for salvation in 9:22, 11:6 and 12:14.
8. Hebrews explains much in the Old Testament that God placed there for our learning. Underline 1 Corinthians 10:11 which says this.

James

Know the book

James was written by the James who was a main leader in the early church (Galatians 2:9; Acts 15:13). He was 'the Lord's brother' (Galatians 1:19), or rather, half-brother, being born of Joseph and Mary. He made no claim to any connection with Christ save that of being his servant (1:1), but instead chose to emphasize his brotherly connection with Christians (1:2).

James was initially an unbeliever (John 7:5), but was converted probably on seeing Christ after his resurrection (1 Corinthians 15:7).

James emphasizes practical religion. It deals with conduct rather than creed. Of its 108 verses, 54 contain commands. Its key word is 'works'. Its theme is 'faith without works is dead' (2:20).

James may emphasize 'works', where Paul emphasizes 'faith', but the two are complementary, not contradictory. They do not stand face to face fighting each other, but back to back beating off common foes. Paul shows how a man is justified in the sight of God by faith; James shows how a man is justified in the sight of man by works. Paul says, 'Neither do I condemn you', and James adds, 'Go and sin no more' (see John 8:11).

James is the New Testament equivalent of Proverbs. It has major themes, but constant practical application. It stresses belief that behaves.

CH. 1 TRIALS AND TEMPTATIONS

CH. 2 FAVOURITES AND FALSE FAITH

CH. 3 TAMING THE TONGUE

CH. 4 FIGHTING FRIENDS OR FOES

CH. 5 PATIENCE AND PRAYER

James 1 distinguishes between trials and temptations. The former are opportunities to take a step up, the latter to take a step down. The latter never come from God (v. 13).

James 2, 3 and 4 show practical religion progressing to cover the three realms of deeds, words and thoughts.

James 5 contains three examples of patience: (a) the prophets in persecution, (b) Job in perplexity and (c) Elijah in prayer. James insisted on a man practising what he preached. In 5:17–18 there is a hint therefore as to why he was known as 'The apostle of the calloused knees'—they became hardened through kneeling to pray so regularly.

The final comment from this practical man is to be engaged in the spiritual work of converting sinners and saving souls (5:19–20).

MARK THESE WORDS

1. Ring the frequently occurring word 'brethren' (it occurs fifteen times in five chapters). Remember why he emphasized this.
2. In chapter 1 ring the words 'temptation', 'trials' and 'testing'.
3. In 2:14–26 ring 'faith' and 'works'.
4. In chapter 3 ring 'tongue' wherever it occurs, and note that the whole chapter agrees with 1:26: an unbridled tongue indicates a vain religion.
5. In chapter 4 the Christian is to sort out sides, and decide who are friends and who are foes. Note the contrasts: world and God (v. 4), proud and humble (v. 6), God and the devil (v. 7), single-minded (implied) and double-minded (v. 8).
6. In chapter 5 ring 'patience' and 'pray' (and similar words). Are you so regular and patient in prayer that you are showing signs of calloused knees? If not, at least kneel down now and enjoy a time of interceding for those on your prayer list.

1 Peter

Know the book

1 Peter is the first of two letters by Peter, one of the twelve disciples. He had calls to friendship (John 1:41–42), to discipleship (Mark 1:16–18) and to apostleship (Mark 3:14). Whatever his early failings may have been, a cold heart was not one of them. Commissioned by Christ to 'strengthen your brethren' (Luke 22:32) and 'feed my sheep' (John 21:17), he does precisely that in this letter.

1 Peter is addressed to 'pilgrims' (1:1) in a world that thought them 'strange' (4:4). Christians are to live 'as sojourners and pilgrims' (2:11), and not think it 'strange' when reaction and persecution sets in from the world (4:12).

1 Peter 1:11 indicates the twofold prophetic emphasis of Scripture, namely, 'the sufferings of Christ' and 'the glories that would follow'. Peter used both of these emphases to encourage Christians to prepare for coming suffering.

1 Peter contains references in each chapter to the sufferings of Christ, demonstrating their 'example' application. It also refers frequently to anticipating the future glory and coming of Christ. In this context 'hope' is used, in 1:3,13,21 and 3:15. 'Glory' is used in 1:7,11; 4:13; 5:1,4,10.

CH. 1 A SAVED PEOPLE

CH. 2–3 A SAINTLY PEOPLE

CH. 4–5 A SUFFERING PEOPLE

1 Peter 1 clearly teaches three truths about prophecies of Christ:
(a) The Holy Spirit inspired them (v. 11).
(b) The prophets did not fully understand them (vv. 10–11).
(c) The prophecies were for 'us' rather than 'themselves' (v. 12).

An appeal for practical godliness commences at 1 Peter 2:11. Lusts may be fleshly, but they war against the soul.

1 Peter 3 contains a difficult passage (vv. 19–21). It is not only in Paul's letters that there are 'some things hard to understand' (see 2 Peter 3:16).

These verses seem to refer to a period when Christ, by his Spirit, appealed to sin-bound people in Noah's time. Any hint of a 'second chance to be saved after death' is certainly not to be taken from this passage; this is not taught anywhere else in the Bible, and a person gambling his or her soul on the basis of these uncertain words would be foolish indeed.

1 Peter 5:2, 'Shepherd the flock', echoes Christ's closing command to Peter in John 21:16–17. Those with such responsibilities should remember that 'the Chief Shepherd' will return to reward eternally (v. 4).

MARK THESE WORDS

1. Ring each 'suffering' (or similar word). Check that the sufferings of Christ are referred to in each chapter.
2. Ring 'precious' in 1:7,19; 2:4 6–7; and 2 Peter 1:1,4. Note who or what is precious each time.
3. Somebody once said that there are a lot of 'bees without stings' in this letter. Ring each word that we are told to 'be' in 1:13,15; 3:8 (three); 3:15; 5:5 (two); and 5:8 (two). 'Be' on the lookout for others, as well.
4. Underline and try to memorize 1:18–19. The 'lamb' was for an individual in Genesis 4:4, for a household in Exodus 12:3, for a nation in Numbers 28:4 and for the world in John 1:29.

2 Peter

Know the book

2 Peter was written when Peter was anticipating death (1:14). 2 Peter reveals that the last concern of Peter concerned apostasy. He himself had denied the Lord, and he is burdened for others, concluding his letter, 'beware lest you also fall' (3:17). In 1 Peter the perils were from without; in 2 Peter they are from within. In the former he deals with suffering; in the latter he deals with error. He combats the first by emphasizing 'hope' and 'glory'; he combats the second by the keyword 'knowledge'. 1 Peter is a letter of comfort; 2 Peter is a letter of warning.

CH. 1 FORGETFULNESS MAY HAPPEN

CH. 2 FALSE TEACHING WILL HAPPEN

CH. 3 FINAL DAYS MUST HAPPEN

2 Peter 1 is concerned with growth. The faith of Abraham, the virtue of David, the knowledge of Solomon, the self-control of Daniel, the patience of Job, the godliness of Joseph, the brotherly kindness of Jonathan and the love of John are all qualities which Christians should be 'giving all diligence' to promote in their lives (vv. 5-8).

2 Peter 1 also stresses that faith is based on fact (v. 16) which was foretold in the prophetic Scriptures (vv. 19–21). Peter indicated that his eyewitness experience of Christ and God's heavenly testimony to him (vv. 16–17) were added confirmation (v. 19).

2 Peter 1 also contains the last of seven references to the Holy Spirit in these two letters. He is responsible for sanctifying (1 Peter 1:2), prophesying (1 Peter 1:11), authenticating (1 Peter 1:12), purifying (1 Peter 1:22), making alive (1 Peter 3:18), glorifying (1 Peter 4:14) and, finally, inspiring Scripture (2 Peter 1:21).

2 Peter 2 warns that, just as in the past there were false prophets among God's people, so there would continue to be false teachers. It is interesting to note his assumption that the office of prophet is replaced by the office of teacher. Greed (vv. 3,15), great claims (v. 18) and ungodliness (v. 19) mark

these false teachers out. The godly can be delivered from them (v. 9), but will never be completely rid of them until Christ returns (v. 9).

2 Peter 3 shows that not only is Christ and his redemption denied (2:1) by false teachers, but Christ and his coming again is also denied (3:4). Opposers overlook the Fall, wrongly maintaining that 'all things continue as they were from the beginning of creation' (v. 4); they deliberately ignore the flood (vv. 5–6) and scoff at the final end (vv. 3–4). These three events are also ignored in today's teaching of evolution.

2 Peter 3 indicates the purpose of the delay before Christ's coming again. Before Christ comes to this world, God is giving an opportunity for this world to come to Christ (v. 9).

2 Peter 3 also reveals that certain Christian writings were already regarded as 'Scripture' in addition to the Old Testament (v. 16). Eventually, when all had been written, they were collected to form the New Testament, which together with the Old Testament formed the complete Holy Bible.

MARK THESE WORDS

1. Ring each time helpful 'reminding' is referred to—three times in chapter 1, and once in 3:1; also note 3:2.
2. Ring each 'knowledge' (or similar).
3. Ring each 'beloved' in chapter 3. In 1:7 we are told to add 'brotherly kindness' to the qualities of our lives. Peter was demonstrating that he practised what he preached.
4. Underline the words which summarize the purpose of this letter: 'Beware lest you also fall' (3:17).

1 John

Know the book

1 John is the first of three letters written by the John who was one of the twelve disciples. He wrote his Gospel to unbelievers (John 20:31) but his letters to believers. His Gospel focuses on Christ, while his letters focus on the Christian; his Gospel evangelizes, while the letters exhort.

1 John contains simple words that any child can understand, but profound thoughts that require concentration from the mature Christian.

1 John addresses 'my little children' (2:1). Its contents are family matters from an aged Christian leader. Two errors were beginning to seep into the church. The first error was doctrinal and denied the deity of Christ. John's Gospel emphasizes that the man Christ Jesus is God; this letter emphasizes that God became the man Christ Jesus. Most wrong views in cults stem from wrong views of Christ. The second error was practical and concerned wrong views of sin.

CH. 1–2 FOLLOWING GOD'S LIGHT

CH. 3–4 EXPERIENCING GOD'S LOVE

CH. 5 RECEIVING GOD'S LIFE

As in his Gospel, John has cycles of sevens. He includes seven reasons for writing:
(a) That they might have fellowship with each other—1:3.
(b) That they might have fullness of joy—1:4.
(c) That they might not sin—2:1.
(d) That they might not be worldly—2:13–17.
(e) That they might maintain Christ's deity—2:21–24.
(f) That they might be kept from deceitful teachers—2:26.
(g) That they might be sure of their salvation—5:13.

1 John contains seven signs of the new birth. Each one contains a reference to being 'born of God':
(a) A practice of righteousness—2:29.
(b) An avoidance of sin—3:9.

(c) A life of love—4:7.

(d) A belief in Jesus Christ—5:1.

(e) A love for Jesus Christ and his people—5:1.

(f) A victory over the world—5:4.

(g) A deliverance from the devil—5:18.

1 John contains seven tests for various views and claims. The author's style of repetition means that some statements are not confined to single passages. The basic tests concern:

(a) True fellowship with God—1:6–7.

(b) True views of sin—1:8–10.

(c) True abiding in Christ—2:3–6.

(d) True views of the times—2:18–19.

(e) True grounds for assurance—3:14–24.

(f) True views and error—4:1–6.

(g) True union with Christ—4:13–21.

The doctrinal error concerning the deity of Christ, and the wrong views of sin were connected. False teachers were maintaining that sin was essentially a fleshly failure, and nothing to do with the spirit of man. They reasoned that it would therefore be impossible for God to become a true human (physical) being. John's final words summarize the Christian truth of Christ's deity, to be found throughout his letter: 'We may know him who is true; and we are in him who is true, in his Son Jesus Christ. This is the true God and eternal life' (5:20).

MARK THESE WORDS

Ring each occurrence of the following words: 'know', 'love' and 'born of God'. You could use three different colours to keep them distinct.

2 John

Know the book

2 John was written by John towards the end of his life (v. 1). 2 John contains two keywords: 'truth' (occurring five times) and 'love' (four times). Those that God has joined should not be put asunder. Walking in truth without love would be hardness; walking in love without truth would be softness; walking in both truth and love brings balance, and is the correct Christian practice.

The fact that John wrote this letter is significant. Paul was the apostle of *faith*; James, the apostle of *works*; Peter, the apostle of *hope*; but John was the apostle of *love*. God chose the one known for love to write about love becoming too soft.

2 John is also significant because it was written to a woman (although some people believe that the 'lady' is a church). She is addressed as 'elect' (chosen) of God, which emphasizes the high estimation of womanhood in Christianity. She was known for her 'children walking in truth' (v. 4), which emphasizes the godly influence of true motherhood. If a man errs it is probably by being 'too hard'; however, a woman is more likely to be 'too soft'. The problem the letter deals with is love being too soft.

True 'love' is the pathway commanded for the Christian, and it is shown by observing the commandments, one of which is to continue in the faith as it was originally given (vv. 5–6). True 'love' will not run after novelties. True 'love' must not help those who do. In the context of the letter, hospitality towards a false teacher (v. 10) and wishing such a person well (v. 11) are to be avoided. In the application of the principle, true 'love' must separate from falsehood and have nothing to do with it.

Vv. 1–6 Truth that unites

Vv. 7–13 Truth that divides

True 'love' for Christ and his truth, when followed according to this biblical instruction, is liable to be accused of being 'unloving', or even schismatic. The devoted follower of Christ must remember:

(a) The man God chose to write this solemn warning was known above all others for his love, age, experience and authority in the things of Christ.

(b) The book is short and affectionate; it is placed towards the end of the Bible, and is an essential part of the Scriptures. This shows that its message can be said briefly, should be said lovingly, may be said lastly, but must be said definitely: the faithful Christian must not co-operate with, or help the cause of anybody who is not faithful to Christ and his gospel (vv. 7–11).

MARK THESE WORDS

1. Ring the 5 occasions 'truth' occurs, and the 3 occurrences of 'doctrine'.
2. Ring the 4 occasions 'love' occurs. Notice the absence of the word 'beloved'—in writing to a lady, even an aged man must avoid anything which seems over-familiar.
3. The word 'receive' occurs twice in connection with 2 different things. The Christian can 'receive' one or the other, but not both. Which are you more concerned about?
4. 2 John illustrates the great blessing that can be contained in a brief, loving letter—even though it may be from an elderly person. Check your recent correspondence, and send off a brief, loving letter to someone today.

3 John

Know the book

3 John was written by John towards the end of his life (v. 1). 3 John is a complementary, 'twin' letter to 2 John. Each has fewer than 300 words. 2 John is addressed to a woman; 3 John is addressed to a man. The first is about somebody who was 'too soft'; the second is about somebody who was 'too hard'. In one there is an example of hospitality which is forbidden; in the other there is an example of hospitality which is encouraged.

3 John is addressed to Gaius. The letter commences with a prayer for his good health (v. 2). Older translations say 'I wish' instead of 'I pray'—but it is better to have someone 'pray' that you might be well, rather than just 'wish' that you may be. Those who wish to be spiritually correct in their use of terms today, and replace the word 'wish' with 'pray', should make sure they do not thereby become liars. Paul wished for something he would never have prayed for in Romans 9:3.

It is interesting to note what the 'wish' was. John wanted the physical health of Gaius to match his spiritual health. If that happened today there might suddenly be a lot of cripples around! It is certainly good to be healthy in both body and soul, but a healthy soul in a sick body is to be preferred to a sick soul in a healthy body.

3 John indicates that Gaius may have been converted by John—see the context of 'my' in verse 4.

3 John teaches that the Christian church and Christian preachers should be independent of the world financially—see verse 7.

3 John reveals that Christians can help 'the truth' by helping those who preach 'the truth'.

3 John sadly raises the problem of the domineering, autocratic leader who has turned up in all ages to curse the Christian church. The empire builder in early times was Diotrephes—see verse 9.

'Pre-eminence' (v. 9) is not necessarily a sin—but love for it is. John once wrongly desired it (Matthew 20:20–21). The only other use of the word in the New Testament reveals the identity of the only person who should have it (Colossians 1:18).

The leader in 3 John who loved to have the pre-eminence had seven faults:

(a) He loved the limelight.

(b) He wanted to have everything his own way.

(c) He refused outside help from God's preachers.

(d) He refused to circulate the letters they sent.

(e) He engaged in a criticism campaign to stain their characters.

(f) He told church members who wanted to support them that they were forbidden to do so.

(g) He got rid of those who disagreed with his policy.

Have you ever met a modern equivalent of Diotrephes? These people sadly demonstrate that it is not only doctrinal error that can split churches.

3 John concludes on a happier note; in verses 5–8 he deals with a receiving brother, in verses 9–11 with a rejecting brother (if he was a brother!—see v. 11), but ends in verse 12 with a recommended brother, Demetrius. Make sure you always finish tragic conversations on a similarly happy note.

Vv. 1–8 THE HOSPITABLE SAINT

Vv. 9–11 THE AUTOCRATIC LEADER

Vv. 12–14 THE COMMENDABLE BROTHER

MARK THESE WORDS

1. Ring each 'truth' and 'beloved' (note this is now addressed to a man, whereas it was omitted when writing to a woman in 2 John).

2. Underline John's greatest joy; also underline his greatest wish and prayer for Gaius.

Jude

Know the book

Jude was written by the 'brother of James' (v. 1). He described himself as the 'bondservant' of Christ. Like his brother James, there is no other claim of relationship with Christ (see comment in 'Know the book' introduction to James).

One Judas may have renounced the faith; this one earnestly contended for the faith. There should be no superstition about a name.

Jude is the apostle of *warning*. Paul, Peter, John and James were the apostles of faith, hope, love and good works. Jude warns against apostasy, which can destroy faith, hope, love and good works.

Jude intended to write an explanation of the faith, but need turned him instead to write an exhortation to defend the faith (v. 3). His book could be called 'The Acts of the Apostates', for it deals with apostasy from before the beginning of human history until the return of Christ in glory.

Jude refers to three groups who apostatized:

(a) The angels—known for their rebellion (v. 6).

(b) The Israelites—known for their unbelief (v. 5).

(c) The inhabitants of Sodom and Gomorrah—known for their sexual immorality and perversion (v. 7).

Jude refers to three individuals who exemplified apostasy (all referred to in v. 11):

(a) Cain—known for his self-righteous, 'bloodless' religion.

(b) Balaam—known for his greed for gain in religion.

(c) Korah—known for his presumptuous rebellion in religion.

Jude has many cycles of threes where John often used sevens. Besides the three groups and three individuals, the book has:

(a) Jude ... servant ... brother ... (v. 1).

(b) Called ... sanctified ... preserved ... (v. 1).

(c) Mercy ... peace ... love ... (v. 2), etc.

Jude initially urges his readers earnestly to contend for 'the faith' which was 'once for all delivered to the saints' (v. 3). Revelation is 'once for all time and now completed'. Christians should contend for the historic faith, not new ideas. 'Contending' should be carried out earnestly, but not furiously.

Jude reminded them of prophetic Scripture as a basis of belief (vv. 5–7), and places apostolic teaching on an equivalent level (vv. 17–18).

Jude ended his letter on a personal and practical level. Verses 20–23 show that true disciples are known for:

(a) Building themselves up spiritually.
(b) Praying effectively.
(c) Keeping themselves in God's love.
(d) Looking for Christ's return.
(e) Loving the lost.
(f) Saving the sinner.
(g) Hating their sin.

The final two verses of Jude are popularly used as a 'benediction' in Christian services.

Vv. 1–3 Defenders of the faith

Vv. 4–19 Deniers of the faith

Vv. 20–25 Disciples of the faith

MARK THESE WORDS

1. Ring each 'keep' (it occurs three times). The final 'benediction' contains it; note it also in the opening verse in a different form. We who are 'kept' should make sure we 'keep' the faith (v. 3) and 'keep' ourselves faithful (v. 21).

2. Ring 'ungodly' (it occurs six times).

3. Try to spot other cycles of three.

Revelation

Know the book

Revelation was written by the aged John imprisoned for his Christian faith on the isle of Patmos (1:9). It contains no trace of any grumble because of what he suffered. The book is full of the glory of what he saw.

Revelation is a splendid and fitting conclusion to the Bible. The 'Paradise Lost' in Genesis is restored in Revelation. The Bible started with man being driven from his earthly home and concludes with redeemed man being welcomed into his heavenly home.

Revelation deals with the *future unveiled*. Its subject is the One referred to as 'The Lamb'—the Lord Jesus Christ. He who was prophesied in Genesis 22:8, typified in Exodus 12:5–6, identified in John 1:29, and crucified as described in Isaiah 53:7, is now glorified in Revelation 5:6, magnified in Revelation 5:12, and satisfied in Revelation 19:7 and 21:9. Revelation is the only book in the Bible with a specific blessing promised to each one who reads it and keeps its sayings (1:3).

Revelation is a book of prophecy. Its symbolism appeals to the imagination rather than to the intellect; it is out to promote hope and anticipation in the hearts of believers, rather than visualization in their minds. Different interpretations should be held humbly. The only dogma it is safe to maintain is that unwarranted dogmatism should be avoided. Somebody well said, 'In interpreting symbolism the first critical requirement is constraint.'

Matthew Henry wisely remarked concerning chapter 6: 'Now we are to launch into the deep, and our business is not so much to fathom it, as to let down our net to take a draught.' That advice is excellent for the devotional reader of this book.

Revelation contains much that has been fulfilled in preliminary measure, though final fulfilment is still awaited. Revelation 1:19 gives three statements which help to categorize the contents of the book.

CH. 1 THE THINGS SEEN

CH. 2–3 THE THINGS WHICH ARE

CH. 4–22 THE THINGS WHICH SHALL BE

Revelation chapter 1 contains the vision of Christ which overwhelmed John (v. 17). Revelation chapters 2–3 describe the state of the seven churches at that time, and typically of different churches in different places at different times: the backslidden church, the martyr church, the compromising church, the lax church, the weak church, the favoured church and the lukewarm church.

Revelation 4 contains the song of creation; chapter 5 contains the song of redemption. The Lamb is 'in the midst' (5:6).

Revelation 6 starts various sequences of sevens. It would seem that each 'seven' is chronological, and each new 'seven' describes the same period, so that the book is not to be viewed as in rigid chronological order, but rather as containing chronological cycles.

Revelation has seven churches (ch. 2–3), seven seals (ch. 4–7), seven trumpets (ch. 8–11), seven persons (ch. 12–14), seven bowls (ch. 15–16), seven dooms (ch. 17–19), and seven new things (ch. 20–22).

The final chapter contains a final warning (don't add to or take away from Scripture, 22:18–19), a final promise ('Surely I am coming quickly', v. 20), a final prayer ('Even so, come, Lord Jesus', v. 20), and the final benediction (v. 21). The Old Testament may have concluded with the word 'curse', but praise God that his final words are of blessing through Christ. Amen!

MARK THESE WORDS

1. Ring each 'Lamb' (it occurs 27 times), and each different name of Christ (25).
2. Ring each 'seven' (54 times), and underline the seven beatitudes ('blessed's) to be found in the book.

The New Testament

Conclusion

The twenty-seven books of the New Testament complete the Scriptures God has given to this world.

The final warning given in the Scriptures is:

I testify to everyone who hears the words of the prophecy of this book: If anyone adds to these things, God will add to him the plagues that are written in this book; and if anyone takes away from the words of the book of this prophecy, God shall take away his part from the Book of Life, from the holy city, and from the things which are written in this book (Revelation 22:18–19).

When the Old Testament closed, there followed centuries of prophetic silence in which there was no new revelation. That silence was broken by the coming of Christ.

The New Testament has now closed. There have followed centuries of prophetic silence. That silence will not be broken by new revelation. The next item on God's agenda is the Second Coming of Christ to earth in glory.

Before you start to read the Bible again, try to answer the following questions:

(a) Where in the NT do we read the parable chapter?

(b) Where in the NT do we read the crucifixion chapter?

(c) Where in the NT do we read the love chapter?

(d) Where in the NT do we read the resurrection chapter?

(e) Where in the NT do we read the faith chapter?

(f) Where in the NT do we read the heaven chapter?

(g) Which Gospel in the NT frequently uses the words 'I am'?

(h) Which two books in the NT deal mainly with 'justification'?

(i) Which book in the NT frequently uses the word 'Lamb'?

(j) How do the final words in the NT contrast with the last word in the OT?

Bible Panorama
Enjoying the whole Bible
with a chapter-by-chapter guide

GERARD CHRISPIN

672PP HARDBACK

ISBN 978–1–903087–98–5

A unique introduction to and survey of the Bible, giving an overview to each book of the Bible and taking into consideration the message of each verse, without actually being a verse-by-verse commentary, this book provides a series of very memorable outlines for each chapter of the Bible. It also includes a succinct but vigorous defence of the Bible, concluding with a number of reading schemes to guide the reader through the Scriptures.

Gerard Chrispin is a lawyer also qualified and experienced in management. He has travelled widely on both sides of the Atlantic and in Europe. He is author of three other evangelistic booklets, and of the books *The resurrection—the unopened gift*, and *Philippians for today*, all published by Day One.

'The Bible Panorama is going to really open eyes to the message of this powerful book.'
GEORGE VERWER

'I am enthusiastic about this book.'
STUART OLYOTT

GERARD CHRISPIN

THE BIBLE PANORAMA

Enjoying the whole Bible with a chapter-by-chapter guide

Day One

'Gerard Chrispin has assembled helpful overviews of every passage of Scripture, with clear outlines, that will give you a better grasp of Scripture, no matter where you are in your spiritual journey.'
PHIL JOHNSON, EXECUTIVE DIRECTOR, GRACE TO YOU, CALIFORNIA

Reading your Bible
A starter's guide

GAVIN CHILDRESS AND AUDREY DOOLEY

112PP PAPERBACK

ISBN 978-1-903087-41-1

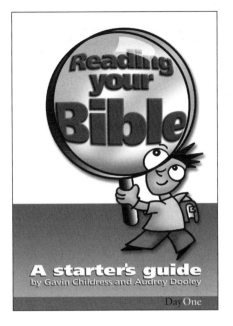

The Bible is the best known book in the world. Sadly, although most people have one at home, it often remains on the shelf unread. This short book outlines key details and facts of each book of the Bible. Illustrated throughout with fun pictures and diagrams.

Gavin Childress has been a pastor at Grace Baptist Chapel, Tottenham, North London, since 1987. He has always enjoyed introducing people to the Bible and has been involved with children's work since his teens. He and his wife Kathy have five children. Audrey Dooley has a BSc and PhD in science from University College London. She has been a member of Grace Baptist Chapel, Tottenham, since 1989. Audrey has been particularly involved in children's ministry for twelve years.

PAUL E. BROWN

128PP PAPERBACK

ISBN 978–1–903087–80–0

How are you getting on in reading your Bible? Do you find yourself reading certain books quite frequently but others hardly at all? Or perhaps you regularly plod your way through the whole Bible but quite frankly find some books very difficult to understand? This is a book to help you!

Paul Brown is the pastor of Dunstable Baptist Church. After studying at London Bible College, he became an assistant pastor and has been in the pastoral ministry for some forty years. He has engaged in further studies with the Evangelical Theological College of Wales, and serves on the Theological Committee of the Fellowship of Independent Evangelical Churches. He is married with three children and five grandchildren.

PAUL BROWN

Understanding and Enjoying the Bible

DayOne